T0078147

Through the Valley

Surviving a Loved One's Suicide

LORI CLANCY

WESTBOW
PRESS®
A DIVISION OF THOMAS NELSON
& ZONDERVAN

Copyright © 2017 Lori Clancy.

THE HOLY BIBLE, NEW INTERNATIONAL VERSION®,
NIV® Copyright © 1973, 1978, 1984, 2011 by Biblica, Inc.®
Used by permission. All rights reserved worldwide

All rights reserved. No part of this book may be used or reproduced by
any means, graphic, electronic, or mechanical, including photocopying,
recording, taping or by any information storage retrieval system
without the written permission of the author except in the case
of brief quotations embodied in critical articles and reviews.

WestBow Press books may be ordered through
booksellers or by contacting:

WestBow Press
A Division of Thomas Nelson & Zondervan
1663 Liberty Drive
Bloomington, IN 47403
www.westbowpress.com
1 (866) 928-1240

Because of the dynamic nature of the Internet, any web addresses or
links contained in this book may have changed since publication and
may no longer be valid. The views expressed in this work are solely those
of the author and do not necessarily reflect the views of the publisher,
and the publisher hereby disclaims any responsibility for them.

Any people depicted in stock imagery provided by Thinkstock are
models, and such images are being used for illustrative purposes only.
Certain stock imagery © Thinkstock.

ISBN: 978-1-5127-8220-2 (sc)
ISBN: 978-1-5127-8221-9 (hc)
ISBN: 978-1-5127-8219-6 (e)

Library of Congress Control Number: 2017905138

Print information available on the last page.

WestBow Press rev. date: 04/25/2017

To
my dad,
the Laughton family, and
all the families who are hurting

Contents

Introduction

My Story

October 5, 1998, was a terrible day, one that would forever change my life. It was one of the worst work days I had ever had. I was a supervisor of a residential program for developmentally delayed adults. An autistic client was so out of control that she bit a full soda can until it burst. Because this client was having such a bad day, I was called back into work later that evening. My staff's interventions were not working.

I was at work at eight o'clock that night when my husband showed up crying. My husband is a typical guy—he doesn't cry much. We had been married for two years at the time, and crying was something that he had almost never done. Something was terribly wrong. He took me outside, looked me in the eye, and said, "Your dad died." I said, "Did he have a heart attack?" He said, "No. He committed suicide." Everything stood still. I burst into tears and collapsed into my husband's arms.

I wish you could have known my dad. He was a simple, hardworking, relaxed man. He was a roofer. He enjoyed cutting wood, watching the Phillies play baseball on TV, eating a good steak, and napping on his favorite recliner. He served in the army in Vietnam. He loved mowing the grass. He loved going to his favorite diner to eat. He also loved drinking coffee, especially at Dunkin' Donuts. He loved cars, grilling out, and working. By all accounts, he was a regular American guy.

He was a good dad. He taught me how to drive. He supported everything I did. He drove me around to all my band practices and youth events. He provided for me financially until I got married. He was also a wonderful grandfather. He loved spoiling his granddaughter.

What we didn't know at the time is that there was more to Dad that either we didn't see or he hid well—or maybe he didn't see it either. In hindsight, I can see that he was depressed. It was nothing out of the ordinary for a lot of guys his age, but things can add up. He was getting older and could not physically do his work as well or without being in pain, so his business probably was not what it could have been. Change was difficult for him, so he did not switch to newer techniques that could have helped him do his job easier. I was married and on my own, living several states away. My brother had just gotten married six months prior to Daddy's dying. Maybe he thought he wasn't needed as much. Maybe he felt he had lost his purpose and value. I really will never know. I could spend years trying to get inside his head, but really all I can do is speculate.

Statistically, my dad fell into a lot of risk categories. He was a married, fifty-one-year-old Caucasian male with no hobbies and limited social support. There is probably some history of mental health issues in his family background (most people did not talk about these things then). He was at the empty-nest syndrome stage of life. Business and culture were changing around him, and he struggled to adapt. He was not one to talk about his problems or ask for help. He had to be tough. He did not share emotions. As I look back on it, he seemed quiet. I thought he was content, but there was probably much more under the quiet, relaxed demeanor.

Since my dad died, I have spent my life helping people. I have been a child care worker in children's homes and a therapist working with people with a variety of problems, from depression to addiction. I have also worked in emergency mental health services for several years, intervening when people are suicidal, homicidal, or in need of detox. I have talked to a lot of depressed people, suicidal people, and people generally in crisis and have had the privilege of walking people through the worst parts of their lives and coming out on the other side. Through the years, I have thought about my dad and those last moments before he died. While I will never know exactly what was going on in his head in the moments leading to his decision, I know my dad was hurting. He was in pain—a deep pain he could no longer live with.

Over time, I have realized I am not alone. There are a lot of us survivors out there, people who have lost loved ones by their own hands. We have struggled with guilt, anger, frustration, pain, and loneliness; we have grieved for time lost and dreams unfulfilled. We have questioned our words, actions, thoughts, and—worst—things we did not do. We have regrets, now painful memories and dreams unfulfilled. We wish we could have one more chance to intervene. We wish we could at least have one more chance to say goodbye or to have one more memory. How I wish I could hear my dad's story, to really listen to what was going on in his heart that day he decided to leave us.

Now, I want to share my story. I want to share how I got through this darkness, finding healing and peace. I wanted to share hope. We survivors can heal. We can overcome. We can move forward. Even while things are dark, there is *light*. The journey is hard, but peace is possible.

This book is dedicated to all of us who have lost a loved one to suicide.

Chapter 1

The Painful Reality of Suicide

Suicide is not a topic people want to talk about. It is not a popular topic at parties and usually ends the conversations it enters. Mental illness still carries so much stigma in our culture today. I want to have this conversation because suicide, mental illness, and addiction affect all of us every day. Mental illness exacts a terrible cost on our society through lost wages and changes in work productivity and relationships. Individuals, families, and communities have experienced lost relationships, broken dreams, and unfulfilled goals. So let's start having this conversation. Maybe—just maybe—if we start talking about the problem and looking at solutions, people like my dad can have hope; they can believe that their situations are not hopeless. Maybe, if we have this conversation, people who struggle every day with mental illness and addiction can have the resources they need to recover and live in peace and fulfillment. Let's have a conversation so we can have a positive impact on some sobering statistics.

Reports from the American Foundation for Suicide Prevention include the following notes:

- Suicide is the tenth-leading cause of death in the United States.
- 42,773 people die from suicide every year.
- For every completed suicide, twenty-five people attempt suicide.
- On average, there are 117 suicides each day in America.
- Men die by suicide at a rate 3.5 times greater than women.
- The rate of suicide is highest in middle-aged men— white men in particular. ("Suicide Statistics")

Why Am I Talking about Suicide? And Why Now?

These statistics have hit me both professionally and personally. I am a licensed counselor. I have worked with suicidal, depressed, mentally ill, and addicted people for the past twenty years. I have answered crisis calls of people who are in the midst of contemplating suicide. I have talked with people after suicide attempts. I have seen the desperation and pain of people who want to end their lives. I have intervened with people who were acutely suicidal. However, suicide statistics have impacted me in another, much more personal way. On October 5, 1998, my father became one of that day's 117 suicides. He was 3.5 times more likely to die by suicide than women his age. He was in the highest risk category of those who complete suicide. I know all of that now, but I didn't then. All I knew then was that my life had changed forever, and my heart was broken. While it took time, intentional healing, and purposeful work, I walked through my valley. I walked out of the darkness and into the light. While nothing can bring back my dad, maybe our story can help someone else in a similar struggle. What I have learned over the years, both personally and professionally, is that stories change people. Stories inspire greatness. Stories impact lives. I want to share my story and some of the stories of people I have been honored to work with over the years. (These stories have been altered to prevent identification of the individuals mentioned in them.) My hope and prayer are that through the stories shared here, you may find both hope and healing.

My dad's death was not the only suicide that has impacted my life. Recently, two more tragic losses had a profound impact on our family. This past April, a sweet family lost their loved one to suicide after a long battle with mental health issues and addiction. We have been friends for the past seven years, and our daughters are best friends. I had helped them connect to services over the years. The dad in the family was struggling; we just didn't know how much. He had sought treatment but had not found the peace needed. He made a decision that will affect his family for the rest of their lives. My family went to his funeral that next weekend. Exactly a week later, I was back in a different church for another funeral for a member of our church family. Another family also had lost a beloved husband, father, son, grandson, nephew, and uncle. He was suddenly gone. These two funerals, coming two weeks in a row, impacted me. Something has to change. Children need their dads. Families need their loved ones. Living with mental illness and addiction is overwhelming. Simply lacking the coping skills to deal with life and having faulty thinking for a moment can alter a family's future.

I knew some of what they were going through, but I felt at a loss about how to help them. I wanted a resource to give these families. As a clinician, I can step back and give them all the statistics and information about suicide. As a friend, I can sit and cry with them because I know personally what the shock feels like. But when is the right time? How do I know when to reach out? I felt like if I could share my story, maybe it could help. Everyone's grief journey is personal, but maybe one day, they can pick this book up and read, process, cry, grow, and—hopefully—begin to heal. I hope to honor their loved ones whose lives ended far too soon. I hope to honor my dad as well.

Suicides are different from other deaths. If a loved one dies from cancer, heart disease, or a car accident, the death is tragic, but most people sympathize. But when we say our loved one died from suicide, we stop the conversation. People do not know how to respond, and we feel more isolated and more alone. People fight for a cure for cancer. Do we fight with such passion for a cure for suicide, mental illness, and addiction? Here is a thought. All three are tragic and can be treatable. I lost a father to suicide and more recently a father-in-law to cancer. Both deaths have been difficult for our families. But someone's choosing to leave can leave a vacuum in your soul. I had a beautiful opportunity to say goodbye to my father-in-law, but my dad robbed me of that opportunity. He was abruptly gone, leaving me with a million questions. While anger is a major proponent of most grief theories, I feel like we get a double portion with suicide. We are angry not only that they are gone but also that they chose to go by their own hands. Suicide also can leave us feeling responsible that they are gone.

We Ask Questions

- Was it something I did or didn't do?
- Didn't he know how much I loved him?
- How could she do this?
- What was he thinking?
- I didn't know she was depressed!

Suicide is tough because we really never get the answers to these questions, although we keep trying!

This little book is my attempt to shine some light on the difficult topics that surround suicide, specifically for the families and loved ones left behind. We are survivors of a tragedy. We are in a club of people we never wanted to join. This reality can present a difficult path to navigate. It is overwhelming, painful, and disheartening. I very much want to give hope to families and everyone else who is walking this path. This path is a most difficult one to walk, but we can walk along it together.

> Being confident of this, that he who began a good work in you will carry it on to completion until the day of Christ Jesus. (Phil. 1:6)

Chapter 2

The Big Why

"Why?" is the number one question after a suicide. It is the question that we seek to answer in the days after our loved one has died. It is the question that plagues survivors for years. It is the one thing we would ask if we had an opportunity. Each one of us will speculate about the reasons behind a suicide. Unfortunately, this question rarely can be answered. The reality is that this one question, more than any other idea, thought, or question, can paralyze us and drive us to the breaking point. At the end of the day, we really won't be able to answer it with any certainty, and spending too much time on it will only slow our healing.

In my years of working with people who struggle with mental health, addiction, and suicide and in pondering this question personally concerning my dad, I have come to understand that there are categories of reasons. Within these categories can be contributing factors that lead up to someone's contemplating and completing suicide. None of these reasons really gives us peace, yet I always have believed that with knowledge comes understanding.

Mental Health Problems

People with mental health problems likely have some defect in the *functionality* of their brains. Because of this defect, they often do not see the world or interact with the world in the same way as you or I do. Activities or events that are normal, natural, and even fun for most are difficult and even dangerous for them. For example, a buffet dinner offers enjoyment and pleasure to most of us; for someone with an eating disorder, it is torture, pain, and agony. Amusement parks and thrill rides can be so much fun, but for someone with panic disorder, they are a terrible experience. Or Wal-Mart, for most of us, it is just a place to go to get laundry detergent and toilet paper, but for so many, it is a place of danger, crowded with people, and a major trigger for anxiety, paranoia, or social phobias. Being quiet in a waiting room is normal social behavior unless you have attention deficit hyperactivity disorder (ADHD), in which case being quiet and stuck in a seat with nothing to do is equivalent to a torture chamber. People who suffer from mental health problems have legitimate disorders or illnesses. These are disorders that we cannot see or may not have medical tests to identify. These illnesses are not visible on the outside but are evident in how people live their lives. Many live undiagnosed for years and learn to mask these struggles. For many people, admitting that they have problems is a serious issue of pride. Thus, most people don't ever share how often they struggle or how deep their problems extend. As a society, we still are not embracing or acting helpfully toward people with mental health struggles, but we are slowly getting better.

Often, someone struggling with suicide has a mental health disorder that may be known or unknown. This does not mean that every person who commits suicide has a mental health disorder. For those getting treated, the treatments are often difficult. Many antidepressants actually increase the risk of suicide because, initially, when the medication is stabilizing in the body, people actually feel better but are not yet to the therapeutic level. So what that means is that people who are really depressed often don't have the energy to commit suicide. As the medication gets on board in their system, they now have the energy but not the ability to think clearly, so that is why this is such a dangerous time.

Another struggle with treatment is that everyone is unique. Ten people who have major depression could have ten different medication regimens. What works for one person may not work for another. While a diagnosis is a first step to getting someone help, many factors affect the potency and efficacy of medications.

Another issue is that we, as a culture, want a drug to fix us. With mental health issues, people sometimes do have a chemical component that needs to be corrected, but there are also behavioral and thought-processing issues that must be worked through. That is why good therapy is so vital. If I tell myself over and over that I am worthless and there is no point in living, then I will likely become more depressed and even suicidal. I need to correct that thinking, and therapy could help identify my negative thought process and replace it with truthful, positive thoughts. Sometimes that faulty thinking is due to life issues, a poor social setting in childhood, or just a lack of correcting oneself. As adults, it is our responsibility to correct those false beliefs, but people with mental health issues seem to struggle in this area of faulty thinking and beliefs. People who act on suicide may have a malfunction in thought processing or belief systems about themselves.

Life Circumstances

Another general reason that people commit suicide is life circumstances. Something has happened that feels unfixable. This often includes things like a job loss, an illness, a separation, a divorce, a breakup, financial problems, issues with children, custody issues, life changes, or arguments. The circumstance could be anything that a person feels is overwhelming at that time or with which he or she lacks the resources to cope.

Whatever the circumstance is, the individual who contemplates suicide feels that this circumstance is unrecoverable. It feels overwhelming. Many times, people in this situation feel like they don't have any purpose left. I remember meeting with one lady who had just attempted suicide. She was someone from my field who had retired and was caring for her aging parents. Both of her parents had recently died, and she was now alone with no siblings, no children, and no one left to care for. She had no purpose. She was really angry that she was still alive. Her life circumstances, grief, and a lack of purpose were overwhelming to her. She saw suicide as her only way out.

Many people who are just looking at the circumstance cannot see a way around, through, or over it. They have lost hope, peace, and faith that anything will change. They have what I call tunnel vision; they can only see what is right in front of them. As the saying goes, "Suicide is a permanent solution to a temporary problem." This is so true, and it is not the solution we wanted our loved ones to find.

Lacking the Right Skills or Supports

Another prominent issue I see in people who attempt or complete suicide is a complete lack of appropriate resources. It really does take a village to support one another. We need communities. We need resources. Many people feel isolated and rejected. People who complete suicide often feel alone, without resources. Sometimes they have alienated everyone around them, or sometimes they just don't know how to reach out to others. They may feel that they do not deserve the relationships they do have, and they may have pushed people away or not let others know how they were really feeling. Whatever the case, they feel alone, and this often contributes to a feeling of worthlessness.

Another issue is that we really do lack communities in our modern culture. Facebook and Twitter are great, but they cannot provide the true sense of community that sitting in someone's home or going for a walk with an actual person can provide. We need touch. We need positive affection. We need people. We need to help others and be helped. We need to know we have purpose, value, and meaning in our lives. This is vital for each and every one of us. Sometimes we are so busy that we just simply don't notice the hurt and pain in the people around us, even those we are closest to.

Another missing support is fun. In my work with people in addiction and mental health, the number one factor they lack is that they don't have fun anymore in their day-to-day lives. It is important to just swing on a swing set, color a picture, enjoy a sunset, go for a walk, play some ball, build a birdhouse, laugh, lift weights, go for a run, go fishing, enjoy an ice cream cone—just have fun. It is life's simple pleasures that can be so fulfilling. It is the normal day-to-day things we take for granted that make all the difference between surviving, living, and then thriving. Every person needs to have fun. Each of us needs a way to cope when life is difficult. Each of us needs to have that one thing that can inspire, encourage, and bring us peace in the midst of life. We need to laugh, to live life, and to live it to the fullest.

The other big thing is a lack of coping skills. The things we can truly count on in life are problems, stress, and change! We absolutely must have skills to be able to cope with these problems and resolve issues as they come rather than letting little or big issues fester, because then we really won't have resources in place to cope. People let little hurts and pains fester and fester rather than forgiving and moving on. When something big happens, they have even fewer resources. Then they feel truly exhausted all the time. And when they are at this place, it really does not take much to break them. I worked with a lady who had never really developed coping skills. Throughout her life she always felt on the brink. She lost an adult child, and because she did not have coping skills in place, she never really could recover from that loss. Just getting out of bed was stressful for her. Deciding what to eat was so stressful that she just didn't eat. Coping skills were vital, and she just did not have them.

Addiction

Addiction can be another contributing factor in a suicide. Addiction is a real disease, and as we learn more and more about the brain, we learn more and more about what addiction is, what causes it, and how to better treat it. But none of this new information changes the fact that addiction destroys lives. It increases the risk factors that we have already talked about regarding why people complete suicide, but it also actually increases the risk of suicide. People who contemplate and plan suicide often don't act on it without a substance that gives them the edge. When the brain is not functioning right because of a drug, like alcohol, a person may be more likely to act on a suicidal thought than he or she would when sober and thinking clearly. I cannot tell you the countless stories of people who attempted suicide that I have met who expressed a strong desire to die and acted on that desire because they were intoxicated. Sometimes this is accidental. When people mix drugs, are partying, or are intoxicated, one of those life circumstances can happen and they will decide to end it all. If they had not been using a substance, they would have never acted on those thoughts or impulses to hurt themselves. Some substances such as alcohol, marijuana, and opiates are depressants. They actually decrease the chemicals in our brains that make us feel good. So if we are depressed and use certain substances, we will become clinically and functionally more depressed. We are also more impulsive when we use substances. Some drugs can intensify the feelings we were having prior to using them, so if I were depressed and then started drinking, I would become much more depressed as well as intoxicated. This is a very dangerous combination.

In general, multiple statistics suggest that people with mental health problems are two-thirds more likely to have an addiction issue and vice versa. This is a grave statistic for potential suicide.

Lack of Foundation

Another issue that I see is that people today are not really grounded. They feel that they have no purpose or meaning in their lives. As a Christian, I have found my purpose and meaning in life. I asked Jesus to be Lord of my life when I was seven years old. I cannot imagine my life without this foundation of truth, purpose, and passion. No matter what life throws at me, I have a firm foundation that is unmovable and unshakable because that foundation is in my relationship with Jesus Christ. Many lack a strong, firm foundation or, worse, have a faulty foundation that has taught them that they are worthless, unwanted, and unneeded. A faulty foundation can contribute to the thinking that leads people to complete suicide. If I feel that I am worthless, unneeded, or making things worse, suicide seems to be a viable option. In my work, I often hear, "No one would even know I am gone," "They will be happier/better off without me," "There is no point anymore," and "I am worthless." We know that this is so far from the truth. We know how much we need our loved ones, how much we love them, and how important they are.

People of faith struggle with all the potential reasons people complete suicide. People of faith also have mental health disorders, lack coping skills, struggle with addictions and life circumstances, and have cracks in their foundations. People struggle without a community to embrace them and care for them. In all honesty, sometimes the church has caused some of those life circumstances and cracks in the foundations. My caution to those who have lost a loved one to suicide is to work through a personal journey of healing so that a crack doesn't form in your own personal foundation.

While we are never going to have the true, firm answer to the why question, it was likely not just one factor that led to the loss of our loved ones. A combination of many different factors converged to create the perfect storm in our loved ones' lives. In hindsight, those factors are much more obvious now than they were before they died. However, these factors are not our responsibility. Like any decision that is made in life, we are individually responsible for making our own decisions. Usually, we make the best decision we could at the time based on the information presented.

This is a hard thought but one I pray you will embrace. Regardless of what caused your loved one's suicide or what the answers to the why question are, this was their choice, their tragedy, their pain. *Please* don't take up their pain where they left off. That is one of the worst things you could do. Their suffering and pain do not need to become yours. You will be in pain. The key, my dear one, is to remember that in this life we will have suffering. We need to walk through the suffering, not set up camp and live there.

Whether you operate from a faith perspective or not, most people are familiar with Psalm 23, one of the most famous scriptures in the Bible. If you are not familiar with it, please read it. Verse 4 is where I want you to focus: "Even though I walk through the valley of the shadow of death, I will fear no evil, for you are with me, your rod and your staff, they comfort me." You are in the valley of the shadow of death right now. We cannot avoid valleys in this life, but we can walk through them. Your loved one may have chosen to live there, to set up camp and reside in the valley of the shadow of death. You now have a choice; you can put on your shoes, pack up your stuff, and start walking—slowly, painstakingly taking one step at a time—and walk out of this valley. It is so important to put one foot in front of the other and start this journey to healing and recovery. Find the courage to walk through the valley, not to live there.

While you are never going to have a true, firm answer to the why question, I hope this helps to establish your understanding that it was likely not just one factor that led to the loss of your loved one. It was in all reality a combination of many different factors that converged to create the perfect storm in your loved one's life—factors that are much more obvious in hindsight than they were at the time. I have found that education and understanding help in the healing process. Take time to find the answers you need to bring you peace, and begin taking one step at a time to move forward.

Psalm 23

The Lord is my shepherd, I lack nothing. He makes me lie down in green pastures, he leads me beside the quiet waters, he refreshes my soul. He guides me along the right paths for his name's sake. Even though I walk through the valley of the shadow of death, I will fear no evil for you are with me; your rod and your staff, they comfort me. You prepare a table before me in the presence of my enemies. You anoint my head with oil; my cup overflows. Surely goodness and love will follow me all the days of my life and I will dwell in the house of the Lord forever.

Chapter 3

Mental Health Problems—The Basics

There are a lot of myths and misconceptions about mental illness in the media and in the public at large. I want to provide you with basic information on some mental health issues that *may* contribute to suicide. Many people say they struggle with depression or anxiety but have never actually been diagnosed. Some say certain people are just crazy. And my favorite is that the term *bipolar* simply means "moodiness." I have heard so many men say things like "She is bipolar. She is so moody that you never know what she is going to be like. She is up one minute and down the next." Moodiness is not bipolar disease. Like many health issues, mental health illnesses are surrounded by many misconceptions that need to be clarified so there is a clear understanding of what the illness is and how it affects people.

Depression

Depression is more than just the blues. It is, in varying degrees, an inability to function. People may come to work or show up at social events, but it takes so much out of them to just do the basics. Just getting out of bed is difficult. I had one client for whom deciding what to fix for breakfast was so difficult that he just stayed in bed and did not eat. Depression is debilitating and exhausting. It is a serious medical diagnosis; it is not something someone can just get over. Whether it is short term or long term, it is devastating. There are also varying degrees of depression, from mild to moderate to severe and then severe with psychotic features. There is also low-grade, more or less constant depression. For most sufferers, depression comes in episodes. Like many long-term diseases, it can go into remission and then come back. One of the key components in depression is often suicidal ideation (American Psychiatric Association 2013).

Depression is a disorder that many times is organic/biological and can be somewhat hereditary. It can also be triggered by a loss or a life event. To be diagnosed with major depressive disorder, people must have experienced a period of at least two weeks during which they met at least five symptoms of depression that are markedly different from their normal state of living. The level of dysfunction shows a clinically significant change in functioning.

Those symptoms could be the following:

1. Increase/decrease in sleep, increase/decrease in appetite
2. Low mood
3. Diminished interest in things normally interested in
4. Lethargic
5. Feelings of worthlessness or excessive/inappropriate guilt

6. Fatigue
7. Diminished capacity to think or concentrate
8. Recurrent thoughts of death, suicidal thoughts (American Psychiatric Association 2013)

Let's be honest: it is hard to love a truly depressed person. It takes a lot of energy to be around one. You may have done all you can for the person, yet it feels like you are pouring into a bottomless glass. It never fills up. We should not feel guilty about not doing or giving more. Good, healthy boundaries are really important in relationships with people who have severe and persistent mental illnesses. Recognize that, with any illness, the person suffering from it has to put effort into getting better. Treatment ultimately rests on the sick person's investing in the treatment, completing recommendations, and progressively working toward health. You can lead a horse to water, but you can't make him drink. Likewise, you can't will or make someone get better, even though you may try many times.

Bipolar Disorder

Bipolar disorder can be a contributing factor to suicide. There are two basic types of bipolar disorder: Bipolar I and Bipolar II. Bipolar I is more manic driven—people who have it experience periods of mania lasting at least one week. Mania involves elevated energy and mood, erratic behavior, and impulsivity. It can present in many ways, such as anger, aggression, hyperactivity, drug use, hypersexuality, spending, and cleaning. Mania is behavior that is out of control when compared to a person's normal mood. These manic episodes are usually significant and often lead to hospitalization. Bipolar II is more depression related. To be diagnosed as Bipolar II, a person must have experienced at least one major depressive episode for a minimum of two weeks and a hypomanic episode, which is lesser in length and intensity than a manic episode.

The best way I can demonstrate this is through this drawing:

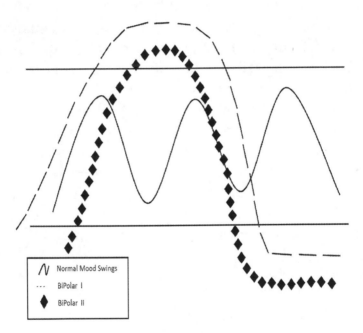

The parallel lines are what is considered a normal range of moods. The unbroken line represents what everyone experiences: good moods and bad moods. We all have that range. The broken line represents what is clinically called Bipolar I disorder. Such a diagnosis means a person has had at least one manic episode that was way outside the normal range and that lasted for at least seven days as well as at least one depressive episode lasting for two weeks that was lower than what most people experience as sadness or depressed days. The diamond-shaped line represents Bipolar II disorder. This is a more depressive range of emotions. As the diagram shows, there has been a hypomanic or a less intense and less impactful episode in a shorter time frame—four to six days—that is still above what most people experience as a good or productive mood. The depressive episode that lasts a minimum of two weeks is again way below what is considered normal mood swings.

Everyone has normal ups and downs and good days and bad days. Bipolar disorder causes extended extremes in that these episodes of highs or lows last for a significant time period. A manic episode is a distinct period of a high, elevated mood and/or anger that lasts for a week that has at least four of the following symptoms:

1. Inflated self-esteem or grandiosity
2. Decreased need for sleep
3. More talkative than usual or pressure to keep talking
4. Flight of ideas or racing thoughts
5. Distractibility
6. Increase in goal-directed activity
7. Excessive involvement in activities that have a high potential for painful consequences (Unrestrained spending sprees, sexual indiscretions or foolish business investments) (American Psychiatric Association 2013)

Again, like depression, this mood is markedly different from the person's normal behavior, and it will affect his or her ability to function. People who experience full-blown manic episodes (and their families) will not forget them. Hypomania (the lesser form of mania) may seem excessive but may blend in better. It is important to remember that mania, hypomania, and depressive episodes are outside the realm of normal. For example, one man I worked with was on disability but went out on a whim and bought a sixty-thousand-dollar truck during a manic episode. Another woman had sex with over fifteen different people she did not know well in a week's time. I knew others who never would have used drugs, but during a manic episode, they used excessive amounts of drugs or drugs they would never consider using normally. When the mania ended, so did the drug use. One client developed and started an entire business by spending seventy thousand dollars in a week's time, renting a warehouse, buying product, and developing letterhead, devastating his family's finances. One can really get a lot done with superhuman energy, little sleep, and no need to eat much for seven days.

Hypomania is a little less intense and doesn't last as long. When people are hypomanic, they can go on a cleaning spree, but when the mania runs out, the closet contents that were emptied into the living room are still a mess in the living room. I had one client who decided to re-side her entire home. So she took all the old siding down, got about halfway done, and ran out of energy. Her house still is not sided because, by the next manic episode, she had moved on to another project. Most people who have hypomania actually like it because they get so much done when they are manic and so little done when they are depressed. Unfortunately, our bodies were not meant to sustain that kind of intensity, so the crash typically comes in the form of a depressive episode. And that is the cycle.

Bipolar disorder can usually be treated with medication and therapy. However, a lot of the medications used to treat bipolar disorder leave people a little lower than even normal (hovering around that bottom line in the previous diagram), and a lot of people like the manic episodes so they often stop taking medications or feel that they don't need them, and then the cycle begins again. Many times, it takes people several cycles of being on medication and off of it before they truly realize the need and benefit of the medication in their lives. Other people decide that they don't like the way medication makes them feel and opt to live with the disease and its effects on their lives.

Another interesting thing about bipolar disorder is that, often, people who are diagnosed with it and have a difficult time with it tend to identify with the disorder itself. When I first got into counseling, I was mediating some groups. In one group for women with mental health problems, there was a lady who had struggled with health and mental health problems all her life. As she was talking, she said, "I have diabetes, congestive heart failure, and high blood pressure; I am bipolar; and I have anxiety attacks." I confronted her on why her identity was wrapped up in bipolar disorder while she just "had" the other disorders. She had never realized that she said things that way. Over the years, I have heard many identify with bipolar disorder as a central part of who they are. Bipolar disorder is a treatable, typically lifelong disorder that people can learn to manage and live with, much like diabetes. What becomes dangerous for people with bipolar disorder is that they come to identify with their bipolar disorder and see themselves as defective and broken. This can become a factor in how they see themselves and a contributing factor leading to suicide.

Schizophrenia

Schizophrenia is a disorder that affects people's thoughts. They struggle with delusions (a false reality) and/or hallucinations (seeing, feeling, or hearing things that are not real). Delusions are beliefs or a distorted reality in which people's minds believe things that are not true or are distorted from what everyone else actually experiences. Hallucinations are distortions in the mind that cause people to see, hear, or feel something that is not really happening. To really understand this disorder from the client's perspective, I always encourage families to watch the movie *A Beautiful Mind* with Russell Crowe. It shows how schizophrenia affects daily functioning and thought processing, as well as what life is like from the family's perspective.

One of the major complications that puts people with schizophrenia at a higher risk for suicide is command hallucinations. This is when the voices in their minds are telling them that they are worthless and should kill themselves. The voices often even tell people how and when to complete suicide or kill others. When the voices bombard people day and night for weeks at a time, they can be overwhelming and difficult to cope with. When people struggle with command hallucinations, they are at a higher risk for suicidal potential. The hallucinations tend to be very destructive and demeaning. However, schizophrenia is also a very treatable disorder with medications and therapy. Medications are often necessary to control those thought patterns. I once completed an assessment in an ER where a man was sitting on the floor. I encouraged him to at least sit on the bed, and he said, "What are you talking about? They are on the bed." When I asked who "they" were, he said, "They are all around me. They tell me I am worthless and to just kill myself. They tell me all the time." He described over forty different people, from small to large, who were in the little ER room with us. After I talked him into sitting on the bed, he was kicked off the bed by one of his hallucinations and fell to the floor. When you cannot escape your own mind, suicide seems to become a viable option.

PTSD

Post-traumatic stress disorder is also a common disorder for people with suicidal ideation, increasing the risk of suicide. PTSD is diagnosed only after someone has experienced a life-or-death situation, such as being physically or sexually abused, a wartime experience, or a severe accident, and is struggling to integrate that event or series of events into his or her daily life. Most people integrate the trauma into their lives and are able to manage their thoughts, feelings, and anxieties. For others, the anxiety increases because of the trauma event, and after six months of increasing symptoms, PTSD may be diagnosed. While it is normal to react to a traumatic event, when the reaction persists or is outside the normal range for that trauma, that is when a disorder could develop.

PTSD is an anxiety-based disorder. The risk for suicide increases when people continuously reexperience the trauma. The traumatic event plays over and over in their minds, like an instant replay that does not quit. People who suffer from PTSD also are hypervigilant about the incident recurring. They may be triggered by random things that remind them of their trauma. I worked with a woman whose husband would regularly sexually and physically abuse her when he was drinking beer. One day "Susie" was walking through the mall and walked by a restaurant where people were drinking beer. Just the smell of the beer sent her mentally back to her bedroom when her husband was drinking and raping her. She ran out of the mall, leaving all her packages on the floor. A couple of months later, Susie was at a friend's house, and her friend's husband popped a beer open. Susie became immediately nervous and started avoiding the people in the room. She began tripping over things. In her mind, she was back in the moment that her husband was doing unspeakable things, even though she was safe in her friend's living room. These incidents can leave people embarrassed, confused, and feeling very anxious.

Smells often trigger memories. Sounds, items, words, even tones of voices can trigger these memories. Fireworks are very difficult for many veterans. Large crowds can also be difficult for many people depending on the trauma they experienced. Car accident victims may not even be able to ride in a car. I had one client who was hit by a car while riding a bike; it took her eighteen months of therapy to be able to get back on a bike again.

Reexperiencing the trauma is often what makes suicide seem like an option. The trauma was so bad, and the person has a difficult time turning off those memories. Or the fear is so great that the only way they see out of their misery is to die. Some PTSD veterans feel guilty for surviving when so many of their comrades died. This is known as survivor's guilt. Many of our military veterans struggle because they came back and their brothers did not.

When someone is so anxious every day, all the time, and their minds are stuck in the worst moments of their lives, suicide looks like an option, but PTSD is treatable, and there is support out there.

Addiction

Addiction to any drug alters brain chemistry and has a significant effect on the individual using the drug or engaging in the behavior. Again, there are very specific criteria someone must meet to be diagnosed with a substance use disorder or the behavioral disorder of gambling. There are three levels of severity based on how many of these criteria are met: mild, moderate, and severe. Any substance can potentially harm someone or cause an addiction. As any person in recovery could tell you, a person's brain under addiction is completely different than when the person is in recovery. Recovery is so important for individuals, families, and communities to support. Healthy, active recovery combats the thought processing that addiction created. No one ever starts using a substance hoping to lose their families, homes, jobs, and relationships. Some people use for years before they become addicted, while some become addicted the first time they use. In many ways, a person struggling with addiction is operating under a brain that has been hijacked. It is not as though you were not important enough for them to stop or they loved their drug more than you. The truth is that many people in addiction hate their drugs of choice. Their brains and bodies are demanding that drug as a means to survival (McCauley 2010). Understanding this is critical for families to know that their loved ones still loved them very much even in the midst of their addiction; they just were unable to express that love in a meaningful or effective way.

Final Thoughts

This, of course, is not an exhaustive list of mental health diagnoses. There are literally hundreds, but depression, bipolar disorder, schizophrenia, PTSD, and addiction are some of the most common diagnoses connected with suicide and suicide ideation in the work that I have done. These diagnoses are also largely misrepresented and misunderstood by our current culture.

If your loved one died from suicide, he or she may have been internally struggling and incapable of ever expressing that to you. Many are embarrassed, proud, or in too much pain to share with others how they are really feeling with those who love them best. The people struggling feel as though they are in prison with a life sentence—only that prison is in their minds. In the heat of the moment, or through months of thinking and planning with faulty thinking, our loved ones decided that the best solution was death. Now we are picking up the pieces. One of those pieces is often the mental health problem with which they were struggling.

Chapter 4

It's Not Your Fault

think every one of us will struggle with these thoughts in varying degrees: *What could I have done differently? Is there something I could have said or done? Is it something I said or did that caused this? Didn't they know how much I loved them?*

We can recount every last word, thought, expression, and memory that we shared with our loved ones over and over again. We replay all the events that happened leading up to our loved ones' deaths. Whether these events are positive or negative memories, we relive them, analyzing, dissecting every word. We desperately try to remember the last thing we said. Asking questions and seeking answers is a healthy part of grieving. Our loved ones are gone, and we want answers. Death is not an easy topic on the best of days, and this? This is the worst of days. We want to know why this happened. We want to understand what they were thinking. There just had to be a reason. Then there's the haunting question we all struggle with—*Was it me? Was it something I did do or did not do that could have made all the difference?* What if our last words were said in anger? What if the last memory is a fight?

One of my relatives, who had a good relationship with my dad but didn't see him often, came to me a couple of weeks after my dad died and said, "Maybe if we had called him and shot pool, maybe he wouldn't be gone." Truthfully, I think he had already made the decision. There was really nothing anyone could have done. Most of us experience regrets when someone dies and we did not have a chance for closure. This is one of the greatest heartbreaks in suicide—our loved ones did not give us the gift of saying goodbye, of ending positively. They chose when to leave and how to leave and we had no choices. And the worst part? We feel responsible.

My Regrets

My father passed away on a Monday. The Sunday before, October 4, 1998, my husband and I were at church like we were every Sunday. It was a really good sermon; it really hit home. Both my husband and I separately went to the altar to pray for my father, something neither of us had ever done before. After church, my husband said I should call Dad. I also felt the Holy Spirit say I should call him. Did I? No. This is my biggest regret. Dad and I were not prone to long, in-depth conversations, so even if I had called him, he likely would not have shared what he was planning to do or how desperate he must have been feeling. But the fact remains that I did not call him. I did not tell him one more time that I loved him, that I was here for him. I did not get that last conversation with him. And of course I wonder, *Would he still be alive today if I had made that call?*

The Grief Process

It is completely normal to ask these questions. It is healthy to process feelings and thoughts as we grieve, but the truth is that, in that moment that our loved ones chose to take their lives, there was nothing we could have done. Many times, once a person has made the choice to die, a serene peace comes over him or her. The struggle is in making the decision. It is not unlike any other major decision you and I make. Remember back to when you were in a difficult relationship. You knew you needed to end the relationship, but you still really cared about the person. You anguished, you prayed, and finally you decided. The struggle is in actually making the decision, not in the execution. Many people contemplate suicide for months or even years. For some, it is a split-second decision; they have immediate access to the means, and they act impulsively. But for most, they plan and experiment. Unfortunately, with all the information on the Internet, we have easy access to just about anything, including how to complete suicide. Many times, our loved ones have attempted suicide prior to this completion. You would likely be surprised by how much your loved one actually thought about this decision. He or she likely struggled longer than you knew.

The Illusion of Control

The truth is that the one thing that you think would have made all the difference likely would not have had the impact you think it would. But we really think it would. I think it is about control. There is so little in a suicide that we as the survivors have control over that we spend time contemplating these regrets of what we could or could not have done. We want to have some control—or the illusion of control. The reality is that we cannot control what others do; we can only control how we react to it. Our loved ones made a terrible, irreversible decision, likely based on faulty thinking and irrational beliefs. Sometimes they formed these beliefs and this thinking over months and years.

One night I was talking to a lady in the emergency room after she had intentionally overdosed, and she shared her story with me. She had struggled with mental health issues much of her life and was currently living with her daughter. She had been homeless multiple times and had been in and out of psychiatric hospitals. She never felt like her medications were quite right. She felt she was a burden to her daughter as she watched her daughter struggle to take care of her as well as her own children. This lady thought things would be much easier on her daughter if she was just gone. In her mind, she was doing her daughter a favor. She didn't realize that she would not just be gone. There is a path that is left behind after a suicide, a path that is very difficult to navigate, and a path that we cannot control.

The Important Truth

I want you to know that this really is not your fault. I know you are going to struggle and argue with me on this. I know this is an area that you will explore, process, and investigate. Again, do what you need to do to grieve, but please don't stay here too long! You are the survivor. You are making a choice to put one foot in front of the other. Keep on moving. You cannot change the past. The decision has been made. As much as you want to have power and control over the situation, you don't. You don't have any power or control over the past. You do, however, have power and control over the present. Focus on what you can change and what you can do today.

I want you to think back to the story of the Three Little Pigs. Each pig knew about the dangerous big bad wolf. Each pig had a different strategy to cope with the situation. One pig built a house of straw. One pig built a house of wood, and the third pig built a house of brick. Each made his choice based on the information he had at hand. At the end of the day, one pig's home survived because of the choices he had made when he was building his home. The third pig was not responsible for the other two pigs' homes. In the same way, we are not responsible for the choices our loved ones have made. We are living with the wreckage left behind. Their choices are affecting us, but we are not responsible for their choices.

A parent of one of the kids in the children's home whose husband died told me something that I will forever remember: "Normal as I know it is gone. I have to establish a new normal." Making something new is so hard, but we can't get back what is gone. That is why we grieve. Grieve, mourn, wail, and get it out. It hurts. It is terrible. I can't make this part better right now other than to say that there really is a greater peace on the other side of pain. Work through this! Take the time to grieve and come to a place where you truly realize what has happened is *not* your fault. What is happening in the present is what you can affect. Be intentional with each moment you have to grieve and heal.

Journal Opportunity

Take a moment to write out any regrets you have. Then, with a trusted friend, pastor, or a counselor, share these regrets. Take the time to process them. As you do and you come to realize that they would not have changed the outcome for your loved one, go back and cross them out.

_____

_____

_____

_____

_____

_____

Chapter 5

Is This God's Fault?

M any times, when a loved one commits suicide, God is the first one to get blamed. We ask, "Why did you allow this to happen? How could this happen?" Then we start making accusations:

- You did this!
- You could have stopped this!
- You knew he or she could not handle _____ (problem that led to suicide).
- If you are such a loving God, you would have stopped this.
- You never healed him or her of _____ (mental health issue/addiction/problem).

The truth is that, yes, God is big enough and all-knowing enough to have stopped this, but he also gave us and our loved ones free will. This is something I have wrestled with many times. Free will is a gift from God to us all, but it is also what causes many of us to fall. Why do others continue to make the same bad choices? Why does so much seem to happen to some people? Why do we have to deal with the consequences of other people's' sin?

When I was younger, I once worked with someone who experienced a heartbreak. She had fallen in love with a young man who had very similar values, aspirations, and vision. She felt they both had given their lives to Jesus and were going to follow him with full-time ministry. She knew this was her purpose and her calling. She was grounded in her faith and thought he was too. They were engaged and planning a wedding. Then, several months into the engagement, he came to her and said he was in love with someone else and wanted to sell shoes. He left town, and she lost contact with him. Afterward, she felt lost. She felt she could not do what God had called her to do without a mate. She wondered aloud, "What happens to the faithful people left behind when someone doesn't follow what God has called them to do?"

While her situation is different from a suicide, the question is still the same: What do we do when someone exercises their free will against God's best and then that decision affects the ones left behind?

Free Will vs. God's Best

Through the years, I have heard similar stories. I have prayed, read scripture and came to some conclusions.

1. Suicide is not God's best for anyone.

    When God creates a person, he has a purpose and a plan for that person from the moment of conception (Ps. 139, Jer. 29:11). God gives us passion, value, and meaning. God created us in his image (Gen. 1:26). He created us for a relationship with Him and with others. It is our job to discover what that purpose is and live that purpose to the fullest. Suicide abruptly ends that process of discovery. Even in Samson's case, God's desire for Samson was to fight for the Israelites. When Samson gave in to sin and lost his strength, he lost his God-given purpose. Samson prayed for strength one last time, and God granted that request. Samson's suicide was not God's best for him; living life in obedience, truth, and integrity was God's best (Judg. 13–16).

2. God has the power to stop anyone from doing anything at any time.

   God is omnipotent. He is all-powerful. The Bible speaks repeatedly about God's power, might, and strength. God can stop anything, anytime, but he does not exercise this right haphazardly. He works and moves intentionally, patiently, and lovingly.

3. God also gave us free will to choose him and to make choices in our lives.

   God will not interfere in our free will. Free will is God's gift to us. It is also what causes pain in life. We are affected by what others choose. This choice is evident from the first pages of the Bible. In Genesis 3, God had provided that first choice. He created us without sin, and he then gave us a choice. "But God did say, 'You must not eat fruit from the tree that is in the middle of the garden, and you must not touch it, or you will die'" (Gen. 3:3). God clearly set his expectation and clearly explained the consequences if Adam and Eve did not obey. They knew the choice. They knew the consequences. God honored his own word.

4. Sin is real, and it is a struggle.

    Romans 7:14–20 describes the struggle of sin. We do not do the good we want to do because of the power of sin over us. We end of up doing the things we do not want to do. The struggle is real: If sin were not such a struggle and not difficult to overcome, then it would not have power over us. But the truth is that sin is powerful and is a struggle to overcome.

So, yes, many times there is a direct conflict between God's will and our choices. Because God is sovereign, he knows ahead of time what we will do. Because of his gift of free will, he does not interfere. He allows us to make choices every day. Sometimes we choose wisely; sometimes we don't. Either way, we experience the consequences of these choices. This is where the problem is; all of us, at some time or another, have blamed God for the consequences of choices we make. Do we also blame God for the choices that others make? It is a totally natural thing to do. We are grieving, hurting, and experiencing pain to the depths of our souls, a pain that we never thought we would ever experience. God feels like the right person to blame. It has to be his fault. Free will really is a necessary gift that God has given us, even if at times we do not like the results of our choices and the choices of others.

The Beauty of Being Chosen

Without free will, we would be little robots doing what God told us to do. That is not why God created us. He created us to have an intimate relationship with him. As hard as the terrible twos and teen years are, we would not want little robots for children. Yes, it would be much easier, calmer, and more peaceful, but they would not be choosing a relationship with us. As parents, we want relationships with our children. We spend time with them, train them, and guide them, and when they are grown, we hope they continue to want a relationship with us. The sweetest moments in life are those when someone chooses you.

Everyone loves to hear of marriages that last fifty, sixty, or seventy years because they know such a couple had to keep choosing each other to make it work. That is true love. God wants the same for us. He wants us to choose him and to keep choosing him. He did not want robots. He wanted a loving relationship with us, so he gave us free will. That means, though, that there will be people who do not choose him. There will be people who choose him and then reject him. Sometimes people will reject him repeatedly. We are the same. There will be people who make painful decisions that have terrible consequences on the ones they love most.

Just as God is hurt, saddened, and pained by the choices of others, we are made in his image, so we will feel this pain.

Is our loved one's suicide God's fault? Well, he created free will and gave it to us. Sometimes people's exercise of free will hurts us terribly. So I guess that, at the end of the day, you could argue that this is God's fault. But would you really want a world without free will? It sure would be neater and cleaner and have a whole lot less conflict. But just as I love it when my little girl or boy runs into my arms and says, "Mommy, I love you!" God wants us to run into his arms and cry out, "Daddy, I love you!"

Maybe today, that is where you need to start. Tell God that there is so much you don't understand right now about why you are going through this, and let him hold you and tell you that you *will* get through this. Let your tears fall on him. He loves you so much. He wants you to run into his arms and just be held.

Journal Opportunity

Today, take a moment to write out a prayer to God. Tell him how you are feeling. Then let him love on you for a while.

_____

_____

_____

_____

_____

_____

Chapter 6

God Really Is Big Enough
to Get You Through

To really begin this conversation, I need to ask you a question: What is your view of God?

I want to start with this because the answer determines whether or not you really believe that God is big enough to get you through *this* or whatever situation life brings you. I think going through this kind of loss tends to lead you in one of two directions—you will either run to God or get really angry at God. In situations like a loved one dying from a suicide, at some point you have to have a conversation with God, even if it has been a really long time since you talked to him.

I worked with a young girl one time who was called into the mission field. While she was in school, some repressed memories of her father came flooding back to her memory. She knew that her father had died from suicide, but now her grief was complicated by memories of multiple incidents of abuse throughout her later childhood. She was angry at her dad. She was also angry at God for allowing this to happen.

She thought, *If God is so great, so sovereign, so in control, why did this happen to me?* Why did she have to remember? Her dad had died by his own hand, and she was left holding all the pieces. At the end of the day, for this young lady and for me, the answers come in our view of who God is.

The Name of God

The term *God* really can mean so much in our current culture. Many times, our childhoods or upbringings determine a lot about our view of God. Words like *father, creator, savior,* and *friend* have different meanings depending on where your life has taken you in your relationship with God. For the young girl I mentioned, the term *father* was definitely distorted based on her experiences with her earthly father. It was difficult for her to view God as a loving, faithful, caring father. How you interacted with God and what you learned about him is being tested as we speak. Is God strong? Is he just someone you know from church on Sundays, or is he personal, real, and present in your life? Is God sitting up in heaven watching us like ants on an anthill, distant and aloof? Maybe you have never really thought about this before in these terms. Losing someone we love to suicide will make us really question God and what we believe about him. If he is really in control of all, then *why* did he not stop this?

Ask the Hard Questions

Some people tell you not to question God, but those people have not walked in our shoes. Possibly, their view of God is pretty small. God, the God of the Bible, the Great I AM can handle my questions. When you walk through the valley, this valley, you are going to have questions. I was really mad, even several years after my dad died. I was very angry. I was angry with God. I remember sitting and crying out. If he was sovereign and loved me, why did he allow my dad to die? You will have questions too. One thing I learned through the process of grieving was that it was okay to be mad at God. He really can handle it. He was not going to smite me from heaven for being angry. He is not shaking in his boots because you have a question he may not be able to answer. As I got to know God and through working with lots of people, I realized that anger is not a bad feeling. From a Judeo-Christian viewpoint, we are created in the image of God. God experiences a range of emotions, including anger. God gets angry especially at injustice and sin. Why should we who are created in his image not feel anger? We have lost a loved one in an unimaginable way. It is okay to be angry. And God really is big enough to handle your being angry with him. Anger is also a natural stage of the grieving process. Kübler-Ross developed the five stages of grief; anger is the second stage. It is okay to be angry; it is what we *do* in our anger that gets us into trouble. I had one rule in therapy with clients about anger: "It is okay to be angry. You just cannot hurt yourself or others when you are angry."

That's it. If you follow that simple guideline, it really should keep you out of trouble in your anger. It is okay to tell God you are angry. He really is big enough to handle your anger and your questions.

Who Is God?

So who is God? I cannot answer this question for you, but I can point you in the direction of who God says that he is from his word the Bible. If you are struggling with the concept of who God is, I encourage you to take some time to read these passages from the Bible. These are just a few of the verses that describe who God is and some of the promises he makes to help us when we are hurting. The more time you spend in God's word, the more you will know who he is and understand his heart for his children.

1. God will never leave or forsake you.—Joshua 1:5, Heb. 13:5
2. God is full of compassion.—2 Corin. 1:3–7
3. God understands sorrow.—Isa. 53:3–5
4. God takes ashes and brings beauty.—Isa. 61:1–3
5. God is all powerful.—Isa. 26:3–4
6. God is sovereign.—Isa. 9:6, 25:7–8
7. God keeps his promises.—2 Chron. 6:14
8. God is strength and our shelter.—Ps. 42, Ps. 10:14, Ps. 46, Ps. 73:26, 2 Sam. 22:2–3

I can tell you what I have learned over the years about what God is not.

- God is not angry at you or your loved one. He loves you, and he loves your loved one. His heart is broken. He is grieving with you and for you.
- God is not a genie in a bottle. I think we get this wrong in our current culture a lot. God is not a genie in a bottle that we pull out to satisfy our latest whim or desire. He is not here just to make us happy.

- God is not weak. Many people feel that God can't handle *this* situation. God is God. He is strong, powerful, omnipotent, omniscient, and omnipresent. He has always been and will always be. He created the universe in six days. He raises the dead. He heals the sick. He calms storms. He is the Judge. He is God. He really can more than handle anything.

- God is not a giant whack-a-mole game in heaven. Have you ever played the whack-a-mole games at carnivals or arcades? The little mole pops his head up, and you get a point if you whack him with your club. Sometimes I think that is how some people view God. He is in heaven with a giant club whacking you just for pleasure as you run for cover. God is not out to get you. He is not trying to whack you if you do something wrong.

- God is not distant. Some people say, "He doesn't know what I am going through." They see God as being out there and not down here and feel that he is really irrelevant to their situations here on earth. God is very present with you right now. If you have accepted him as Savior of your life, He is with you right now. Whether you recognize his presence or not is completely up to you.

Who God is or is not to you has to do a lot with your perspective on life circumstances. I know I wrestled with these topics, and I have seen others wrestle with them. Don't depend on someone else to determine who God is to you. Study his word and talk to him through prayer. Really get to know who he is and what his heart is. He knows you are hurting and wants to be your comfort. He loves your loved one too!

I have worked with so many people in counseling, in churches, in hospitals, and in homes who are operating under a false belief regarding who God is. When we go through a suicide of someone close to us, it will rock our view of who God is, or who we have believed him to be up until that point, but before making a decision on who God is, we need to get to know him and who he says that he is. He is big enough to take your anger; to provide you all the comfort you need; to give you peace in this storm; and to provide healing, hope, and love when you are broken, hurting, and in despair. God is who will bring us through this valley of the shadow of death.

Who you believe God is will directly determine whether you think he is strong enough to get you through *this*.

Who you believe you are also will determine if you think you will get through this.

Cracks in Our Foundation

My dad was a roofer, so I grew up going to job sites and learning a little about construction. One thing I know that is true in construction and also with our souls is this: if there is a crack in your foundation and you go through a storm that shakes you down to the foundation, it is likely that the crack will widen. So while you are hurting because your loved one chose to leave you, if you had a firm foundation prior to the death, you will not become broken while you are shaken. If you had a fracture in your foundation because of what you believed or thought to be true, this loss has the potential to break you. That is why I want you to evaluate your personal foundation. Go back and do the healing you needed to do. Maybe you didn't know you had a fracture until this incident revealed what was lying deep in your soul. As I was grieving my dad, all this other stuff came up that I needed to deal with and heal from. Unfortunately, I couldn't grieve my dad properly until I dealt with the other stuff that was getting in the way of my healing. I needed to go back and pour some concrete in the cracks in my personal foundation. I needed to fix the cracks that had been revealed in my foundation when my dad died. My dad's suicide did not cause them; it just revealed them. That is what happens when someone commits suicide. Those left behind are rocked to our cores, and either our foundations are proved to be solid or cracks are revealed. Once we see these cracks and consciously know they are there, that is when it is *our* responsibility to fix or heal these cracks. We cannot go on forever through our adult lives blaming others for our cracks. Someone else may have caused them, but they are still *our* cracks that need to be healed. This is a great opportunity to take the time to heal. Counseling can really help identify these false beliefs in God or in yourself that you struggle with to help you be able to grieve your loved one.

Some false beliefs or cracks that I have come across in working with people are the following:

- I am unloved.
- I am unwanted.
- I am worthless.

- I am broken.
- I can never get better.
- I will never get through this.

These are all potential cracks in your foundation, and they are all lies. Typically, they originate when someone speaks these statements over you or something happens to you to begin a fracture, and you unknowingly begin to believe the lie. Over time, the fracture gets bigger and deeper until it is an integral part of your life. You have lived around it so long that you forgot it was there until now. While it will take longer to go back and heal your foundation, you will be stronger in the end if you take the time to heal properly. It is important to seek counsel to help you along in this process. Seek counseling with a qualified professional for whichever cracks you have uncovered. Whether those cracks are mental health issues, core beliefs, or spiritual issues, seek the appropriate help to resolve them. The amazing thing about grief is that there are guidelines but no road map. Siri will not give you any step-by-step instructions. Your grief journey is yours. You choose to start, continue, and get over the bumps and through the roadblocks to the finish, or you choose to stop living. Your loved one has not made that choice for you; that power is yours. What are you going to do with that choice?

Knowing the Truth

When you understand who God is and when the cracks in your foundation are repaired, you will know beyond a shadow of a doubt that the God of the Bible is really big enough to handle this situation. He will be there every step of the way, whether you can see him and feel him or not. He is big enough to handle your emotions. He is the comforter who can give compassion in a way that you have never felt before (2 Corin. 1:3–7). He alone can provide the peace that passes all understanding (Phil. 4:7). He alone is writing the plan for your life, not to hurt you but to give you a hope and a future (Jeremiah 29:11). He promises to never leave you or forsake you (Heb. 13:5b). He loves you just as you are.

Another question that arises about suicide and God is, 'Is suicide the unforgivable sin?' Nowhere in scripture does God ever state this. It is an unconfessed sin, much like if someone was to suddenly die in a car accident with sins left unconfessed. I would think that many people die with unconfessed sin. In discussing this, some people like to point out the story of Judas. His great sin was betrayal, not suicide. Once he fully realized what he had done, the weight of his sin led him to an impulsive suicide (Matt. 27:3–5). Scripture is clear that if you have a personal relationship with Jesus Christ, then when your time on earth is through, you will go to heaven. If you do not have a personal relationship with Jesus, then you do not go to heaven (John 14:6). Our eternal destiny is not determined by the manner of our death but rather by what Jesus did through his death and resurrection. If our loved ones asked Jesus into their lives prior to their death, then they are in heaven. My brother often thinks about my dad in heaven, whole and at peace, and that gives him a strong sense of comfort and peace. I pray that this truth can give you peace.

God clearly says that the truth will set us free (John 8:32–36). Let the truth of God's word and who he says that you are determine your steps from here on.

Lori Clancy

Journal Opportunity

What have you learned about who God says that he is?

_____

_____

_____

_____

_____

Were any cracks in your foundation revealed as a result of your loved one's suicide?

_____

_____

_____

_____

_____

What is your plan to help you repair those cracks?

_____

_____

_____

_____

_____

Which of God's promises are you claiming to help you today?

_____

_____

_____

_____

_____

_____

Chapter 7

It's Okay to Be Mad, Sad, and Happy—Again

I remember feeling so much for the first couple of years after my dad died. At first, it was complete shock. Then I just needed knowledge and facts. Had someone called right before he died to trigger him? Was it something someone said? Had he been planning it? Was he thinking of us when he died? I just wanted to know. Then my need for knowledge turned to anger. I was just really mad. I had been married for a couple of years and had just started a new job at a children's home. This was supposed to be an easy, enjoyable time in my life. I felt as if I had a huge, dark cloud over me. Intermixed with anger was a deep, prolific, sometimes unspeakable darkness. The word *sadness* didn't quite seem to fit, but I was just sad. Then I would have these moments when I felt joy and happiness. Sometimes I felt guilty for feeling happy, almost like I shouldn't feel happy without Dad.

I am not sure what you are feeling right now. I know that, with this type of grief, the feelings are in great supply and come from various directions. Whatever you are feeling, they are your feelings. Own them rather than running from them. It took me about three years to really get it all out. Life kept going while I was hurting. For me to truly grieve, work through all the emotions, and find peace again, it took a while. As I was purposeful and intentional in my grief journey, then my faith grew deeper.

Grief Is a Journey

One main thing I learned through my own process and helping others through the process is this: Grief is a journey. It is a very personal journey. It is your journey. You will be the only one who can navigate it. But you need to navigate it. A while back, I was working with a girl who was about twelve years old, and she was struggling with the death of her beloved grandfather. She had no idea how to grieve, so I gave her a challenge. I asked her to talk to ten people about how they had handled a loss and grieved. She came back with all kinds of examples, including counseling, talking, and journaling. One man, a lifelong farmer, said that he went out and talked to his cows because that was the best way for him to grieve. They were always there and seemed to listen. Another person I knew would write music. Many find comfort in working out, going into nature, and hiking. I often sat by water and just cried. The noise of the water would drown out my sobs. Water is also very peaceful to me. Sometimes just crying is so therapeutic; crying releases so much from your soul. In other cultures, mourners literally scream, expressing the emotion verbally and loudly. Here again, there is no right or wrong. The important thing is to be intentional and purposeful and to allow your heart to grieve. So many are afraid to let their feelings come. There is so much to be emotional about when we lose someone to death in general. When a loved one dies by suicide, it intensifies all of those normal grief feelings.

Getting Started

It is time to start or continue on your journey. There is not a right or wrong way to grieve, as long as you are doing it. My anger rule also applies here: as long as your grief does not hurt you or anyone around you, go for it! Experiment. If you like to write, start writing. If you like to run, run. If you like to do crafts, go be creative. Channel your grief into something. In my case, I learned to scrapbook. I told my dad's story through pictures and journaling. I ended up giving my scrapbook to my brother as a baby shower gift for his daughter so she would know her grandpa. But making the scrapbook helped me heal so much.

After years of working with hurting people, I have learned some important truths.

1. Emotions are good. They need to come in order for you to grieve. You need to embrace your feelings.
2. Find a circle of friends, family, and counselors. Don't make the mistake of just going to one person; you will burn him or her out! A good grief group can be very helpful because everyone there can relate.
3. Cry, mourn, and wail as you need to. Find times to let it come. You have a lot inside that needs to come out.

One of my fails in the grieving department actually came after we lost our precious Labrador, Hunter. Hunter was our dog before we had kids, so he was like my kid. We walked the lake together. He was my buddy, and I loved him. Hunter was with us for seven years, and then his health slowly declined because of his size (120 pounds). He finally could not walk anymore and could not even get up. He passed away when I had a one-year-old and was pregnant again. I did not have, nor did I take, the time to grieve my dog. Well, about a year later, my husband took me on a date night to see a movie. We thought it was a fun chick-flick kind of movie; it was *Marley and Me*. Sitting in the movie theater that evening, the floodgates opened and my grief for Hunter came pouring out like a river. It was not cute, pretty crying; I was gushing mucus and tears everywhere. It was so bad that the lady next to me gave me her whole pack of tissues. I use this example to prove a point: your emotions are real, they need an outlet, and they will come. If you take the time to feel pain as you are able, you will be so much further along your grief journey and possibly avoid embarrassing movie theater moments.

Grief vs. Depression

As a counselor, I get asked a lot, "When does grief turn to depression?" or "What is the difference between depression and grief?" This is a great question. The best way I can describe grief is that it comes in waves. Just like standing in the ocean, a little wave hits, and then a big wave hits. Everything will be calm for a while, and then a wave hits. That is grief.

Grief will often have a trigger that leads to one of those waves. You may hear a song or smell a particular scent, or a person who brings back a memory may walk by. That memory can trigger a wave of grief over you. Sometimes these waves can bring peace, anger, sadness, frustration, or joy—whatever emotion is connected to the memory. Sometimes these memories become tainted because our loved ones are gone.

Depression is more of a constant low, depending on severity. It feels like you are constantly drowning and can barely catch your breath. When a person is depressed, just doing normal, day-to-day activities can take way too much energy. Someone who has a history of depression who then experiences a terrible life circumstance is at a higher risk of having a recurrent episode. Prolonged, unresolved, or complicated grief can also trigger a depressive episode.

Grief is more episodic, occurring in moments. Depression is more of a constant, perpetual mood. There are ranges of depression, from mild to moderate to severe. Unresolved grief can turn into depression. While experiencing grief, you could slip into a time of depression as well. That is why healing is so important. You need to be aware of how you are coping and actually go through the steps of grief. Depression can actually interfere with your grief process. You can get stuck in your depression and actually not go through the healing process needed to come to a place of acceptance in your grief. As you are self-evaluating, grief is a momentary experience from which you quickly bounce back. Depression causes you to stay in a low mood for days, weeks, or months at a time and feel like you are just hanging on to survive. It is important as you are grieving to keep a balance of grief; work; and positive, fun moments in your daily life.

Also, from a clinical point of view, when we grieve, we should be very cautious about alcohol, drug use, and even over-the-counter medications. In the early weeks after the tragic death of a loved one, you may need medicine to help you sleep and eat to get your body back to homeostasis, or a normal balance, especially if you were the one who found your loved one. You have trauma on top of your loss, and you should be cautious that you are not coping through using substances. This will impede your grief process and will cause more problems than it has ever helped. Alcohol and marijuana are depressants, so if you use them to help forget your pain, these substances will actually make your brain more depressed and will make you more prone to depression while also hindering your grief process. Substances or addictive behaviors will never help the grief process; they only stunt or delay the process altogether and possibly cause more troubles.

Will I Feel Happy Again? Is It Okay to Feel Happy?

Sometimes, especially in the middle of our pain, we need to remember the good in life. Reliving moments of joy in the midst of pain offers a much-needed release. I remember feeling guilty when I laughed or joked, like I was betraying my dad. But laughter helps the soul heal. It reminds us that our loved ones would want us to keep living. It is important to keep their memory alive. They would want us to remember the good times. Even now, eighteen years later, I miss my dad. There are still times when I cry. Most of the time, I enjoy the simple things the way he did, and I find joy in them. Dad would want me to enjoy life. He would want us to go to a baseball game, eat doughnuts, and take the kids to the park.

Our loved ones want us to live, love, and laugh. While the way they left this life is tragic and does leave a sting in the memory, they are now free from their pain. They did not die so that you could pick up where they left off. It really is okay to begin feeling joy, happiness, and peace. Experiencing all feelings is an important part of this journey.

Feelings Come in Packages

One of the things I teach in counseling all the time is that feelings are a package deal. So many people get stuck not wanting to be hurt again that they shut off the bad feelings. They keep people at a distance, thinking they can't get hurt again. Unfortunately, when we shut off fear, anger, and pain, we also shut off love, peace, joy, and contentment. All feelings are important and necessary to live life abundantly. I know that right now you are feeling so many emotions. Your pain is real. The more you love, the greater the pain can be. But keep yourself open to healing, seek counsel, talk, mourn, and grieve, but also seek joy and peace. It will come as you work through the pain; you will heal. There is a tendency when pain is great to shut down so we don't have to experience the depths of our pain. I can never guarantee you won't hurt again, but being isolated and not feeling at all is a far greater pain.

Emotions are a package deal. We must embrace them all. I know you are hurting, and my heart breaks with you. Take the time to acknowledge and feel your feelings, own them, and become comfortable with them so they won't hold you hostage. Your pain is real; it is intense. You can get through this. It is important to embrace the place you are in, but it is also important to work through the pain and reach peace.

You will be able to reach out to people in ways you never thought possible. We survivors have a bond that the rest of the world does not know. We know the tragic pain of a life that ended far too soon. We are not alone. When we let our feelings come, there will be healing on the other side of this valley.

Journal Opportunity

What feelings are you feeling now? What feelings have you been feeling recently?

_____

_____

_____

Have you noticed any signs of your grief turning to depression? If so, it is important to seek professional or spiritual care to help you through this. What is your plan to help you heal from your grief and/or depression?

_____

_____

_____

Have you started your grief journey? Where do you think you are on your journey? What resources do you think you need to move forward?

_____

_____

_____

Chapter 8

What You Will Miss

You already feel the pain of the absence of your loved one. What you will miss will be so specific to whom he or she was and the relationship you had. It will also be specific to the time in life that your loved one left.

The things we miss will be big and small—sometimes insignificant. It might be just a call or a text. Maybe it's eating Sunday lunch or going to a Friday night football game. Typically the things we miss will be the everyday activities that we did with our loved ones. We need to take time to recognize what we will miss and grieve these too. What complicates grief with suicide is that, a lot of times, anger reappears here. The thought that our loved ones chose to leave us and now we will never (fill in the blank) again resurfaces. We are angry that they took the future memories away from us without consulting us.

When we bought our home, it desperately needed a new roof. We were in the path of Hurricane Fran, and Hurricane Ivan was on his way as well. The roof was already leaking and could not take another eighteen inches of water. I was so mad at my dad for not being here. I was mad that it took us twice as long to fix our roof. We needed him. It would have been fun to do it with him. I missed his expertise. But he wasn't here. He made the choice to not be here.

It is also interesting to me that the things we miss are sometimes the things that drove us nuts when our loved ones were alive. My dad went to a specific diner for breakfast and most lunches every working day. When I was growing up, it seemed like a dump, but to him, it was where he hung out and had friends. As a teenage girl, I hated going. Now, I wish I could go have hot chocolate and hash browns one more time with my dad, sitting up on a bar stool at the counter of the diner he loved. My dad also loved to watch Major League Baseball games. He had an uncanny knack to fall asleep in his recliner in the third inning and wake up every time for the ninth inning. What I wouldn't give to walk downstairs in my childhood house to see my dad snoring in his yellow recliner.

I miss my dad. I miss his curious laugh. I miss seeing him endlessly sipping on his cup of coffee. I miss seeing him sitting on his lawnmower, mowing the lawn. I wish I had known how sad he really was. I wish I had known and could have shared in his pain. But that wasn't his way. In the end, I have some great memories with my dad. He wasn't perfect, but he was my dad.

How about you? I know it is hard, but what do you miss? It may be as simple as the person's presence, a smile, a laugh. It may be a certain place that he absolutely loved to go. It might be a song she always danced to or a TV show that made him laugh. Remembering is a part of grieving. There is always good, and there usually is some bad. Be careful to be honest in your recollections and memories. Remember your loved one as he or she was. Remember the love you have in your heart. It is okay to let the memories come.

Here are some ideas to help you remember:

- Design a memory box to keep your special memorabilia in. Make the box special. Put in meaningful things, letters, pictures, and keepsakes that were special to your loved one. Put it out of sight and then take it down when you have time to remember and time for any emotions to come.
- With all the technology we have today, making a folder, album, or some digitally formatted memory book or video is also a great idea. You could make a movie with your favorite highlights from your loved one's life.
- Call a friend and share a memory. Talking about your loved one keeps his or her memory and story alive.
- Go to your loved one's favorite restaurant or coffee shop and order his or her usual. Share a memory if the staff there remembers him or her.
- Do one of your loved one's favorite activities. Whatever he or she loved to do, do it intentionally to remember your loved one.
- Connect to nature. Go for a walk or a hike, and let the memories come. My brother mows grass and lets the memories of my dad come over him.
- Start a journal. There is power in writing things down. Journaling memories is a great way to remember our loved ones. Share funny stories. Write

down how you are feeling through remembering him or her.

As you remember, keep this in balance. It is easy to get stuck in the past. Be sure to pace yourself. Remembering can be emotional, so use your coping skills to ensure that this process is beneficial to you. But also make sure that you remember; it is an important part of the healing process. Always bring balance to the grieving process. Take time to remember while finding that new normal.

You will miss your loved one. I can't make that better for you. Time does help. The more you loved, the more you will miss, but you can cherish the memories. You can celebrate the life you had for the time you had. You can take that person with you into your next chapter of life. When you get angry, do something to get it out in a way that doesn't hurt you or anyone around you. We need to be intentional about healing and be purposeful in remembering. Take the next step forward. It is really what your loved one would want you to do.

Also be ready to share your journey. Remember that you are not alone. Other survivors are out there! You have a story to share. You have someone to encourage you and someone you need to encourage. Your story is important. You have a message to share with the world.

Cheri's Story

Cheri is a good friend of mine who experienced the tragic loss of her husband and her children's father. Gary had been struggling with mental health issues and addiction much of his adult life. He had just come back from a nine-month rehab stay to continue working on his recovery. As a friend, it has been amazing to watch God work in Cheri's life. While she and her family are still working through loss, anger, and fear, God has helped her through her valley with strength she never thought possible. She is now the single mom of an eighteen-year-old son and a fifteen-year-old daughter, and her two youngest daughters are eleven and seven. Cheri wanted to share her story of how God works and what he is teaching her through this season of her life. She knows how important sharing her story is. Her story raises awareness and inspires hope, and she hopes it will give God all the glory. The following is based on an interview with Cheri.

On April 9, 2016, life as we had known it for twelve years stopped. I had not been able to get a hold of Gary for a few days, and as each hour passed without a response to my calls and text messages, a huge sickening hole got bigger and bigger in my stomach. I became nauseous, anxious, scared, angry, confused, and helpless; he never went more than a few hours without calling or stopping by to see the girls.

My daughter began to question why Daddy had not called; I gave my best effort to keep calm and to not let her know I was worried. After we finished eating dinner I sent my son a message while we were sitting at the table together to see if he would go with me to find Gary, and he said he would. I sent my mom a text message to see if she would keep the girls, and she said yes.

It was dark and kind of chilly. As we drove down the road, I prayed and begged God to let Gary be passed out drunk somewhere or gone somewhere with someone. Before we drove up the hill I prayed so hard to God to let us find him passed out. I couldn't breathe as we came around the last curve and came to the top of the hill. It was pitch black except for my headlights. It was kind of cold so I was shivering on top of the sick feeling I had. We found Gary's truck parked outside of his apartment building. There also were not any lights on anywhere inside the apartment and it was silent. My son asked me not to get out of my car and to call a friend who was a sheriff's deputy. I told him to sit still and said I'll run in and look around and I'll come right back out. He wouldn't allow me to go alone, so he got out of the car with me. There are many times now when I wish I wouldn't have allowed him to go with me.

We looked in the truck through the windows because it was locked and found nothing. We called his name a few times and still nothing. I knocked on the door a few times with no response, so I tried the knob and it was open, which was odd; the lights were all off, and he always locks the doors. I reached my hand inside and felt for the light switches. I found them, held my breath again, and flipped on the lights.

Everything was in place—a few dirty dishes on the counter, shoes by the chair, remote on the table, fishing tackle beside the fridge— and then I saw his wallet. I called his name many times, and each time I got louder and the room felt colder. At this point I was still clueless as to where Gary was. I looked in the bedroom where the bed was unmade, which was not normal, and then I saw his phone on the side table. I was stuck; I couldn't move or talk. I began to shake, and my son was talking to me but I don't have any idea what he said. Gary never left his phone anywhere. He had it with him twenty-four/seven, and I began to panic. We went back to the living room, opened the glass door, stepped outside on the deck, and called his name. We used our phone lights to look in the bushes and down the hill, but we didn't find him. My son walked down the path to the creek and looked around and called his name, but there was just silence.

I went back inside and called the neighbor to ask when they saw him last, and they said Thursday, which was the last day we had heard from him. They said his truck had been there since Thursday evening. At this point, we went out to my car and called my friend. I told her the situation and that we had looked everywhere and we couldn't find him. She called dispatch and got the police on the way.

Two deputies came up and started looking around and asking questions. They took information to file a missing person's report. One deputy went to talk to the neighbor, and the other stayed with us. She asked a few questions, and I shared that Gary had battled addiction for almost our entire marriage and had also battled mental illnesses, depression, anxiety, and bipolar disorder. He was not on meds as he had just come home from a nine-month rehab program. She asked me if he had ever talked about hurting himself in the past and I told her yes, but it had been many years since he had brought it up. Then the officer ask if he had ever described how he would hurt himself, and I shared with her what he had spoken about. We went outside to show her where we had looked; I went to show her the only place I had not checked because I didn't have a good light. The deputy shone her flashlight in that area, and then she turned it off and told us, "Go back inside, now!"

I knew instantly why she told us go to in. I heard her radio to dispatch that a body had been found and needed transport to the morgue.

Looking back, I can see that God was protecting my son and I because I had walked in front of the side area, but for some reason I didn't think of using my phone flashlight to look around. I truly believe that God protected us and didn't allow me to think of using my light because He knew what we would find.

In that moment, life stopped! Everything went black and silent. Every ounce of breath was sucked out of my lungs—I couldn't breathe! I felt like I was in a nightmare, and I wanted to wake up so desperately. I didn't want this to be happening to our family. I buried my face in My son's chest and just kept saying, "No! No! No!" I got weak; I just couldn't make my legs hold me up, and I hit the floor sobbing.

All I could think about were my kids—what I would tell them and how they would feel. He left us! He didn't give us time to heal the wounds that had been caused by mental illness, addiction, and the demons that had a hold of him for most of his life. He didn't say goodbye! Our kids and I had gone through so much pain dealing with the addiction and mental illness. Our youngest girls probably did not understand many of the struggles for the previous twelve years. I told the girls when I got home. I was in shock; this couldn't be real. I felt like I was in a dream—more like a nightmare. It felt as if I were watching myself interacting with everyone but from a distance.

For the next couple of weeks, I went through the motions. We had to make arrangements. One of the most difficult moments initially was talking with Gary's mom. She of course was devastated. Gary was her only child, and she was literally half a world away. She had to fly in, thankfully with one of her best friends.

I was in a fog. My children have always been my main concern. They still were my main focus. We had the funeral, which I like to call a celebration of life. When life felt out of control and I was so lost, God was right there. In those first few days, he gave me two verses. He has used these two verses to guide my steps, encourage me, and keep me focused on him in the depths of my pain. The first verse was Romans 8:28: "And we know that in all things God works for the good of those who love him, who have been called according to his purpose." I needed to know that God had a purpose in all of this. I had never felt a strong purpose in my life other than being a mom. I needed to know that God was there.

He assured me that he was. The other verse literally jumped out at me in several places in those first few weeks. Genesis 50:20 says, "You intended to harm me, but God intended it for good to accomplish what is now being done, the saving of many lives." I was almost breathless when I read this. I know that Gary had battled for so long in a spiritual battle. This verse gave me peace that what Satan intended for harm, God would use for something positive. At the time I couldn't imagine what. Now as I look back over the past seven months, I can see the promise and the truth of this verse fulfilled. For a couple of months, I stopped reading at verse 20. But then one day I read further. I needed the promise of the next verse just as much: "So then, don't be afraid. I will provide for you and your children. And he reassured them and spoke kindly to them." I so needed this reassurance. I had not been able to work; our finances were tight to say the least. There was so much chaos left behind when Gary died. I needed to know that we were going to be okay. I needed to know that all the children were going to be okay. Peace filled my broken and aching heart. Tears rolled down my face. In the midst of all the craziness in our lives, God promised to take care of me and my children. And he has.

A lot has happened since that night when we found Gary. I almost feel that I have lived another lifetime in the past seven months. His death has made me step away and look at mental illness and addiction differently. Now I see it for what it is. It makes me want to be helpful to others. There are so many others still suffering. I can see what maybe I couldn't see before. I see Gary so differently now. I see and love the man that God created, not who the world created. Unfortunately, he didn't see who God created him to be. I can separate that now; before, it was hard to see that.

I was so angry that he checked out and didn't fight. But now I realize he did the best he could do at the time. I was angry at him. At times I still battle my own internal anger that I should have done more. So I take those thoughts captive. I say, "In the name of Jesus Christ I rebuke those thoughts, and I take all thoughts captive in obedience to Christ." Every time I pray that prayer, those thoughts are gone immediately. I need to be obedient to him. I have learned over the last twelve years with Gary that my way stinks, and it will never work if it is not God's will.

I have peace, amazing peace, that can only come from God. He has taken away my fear. I know that Gary is in heaven. I know that he is not battling or struggling anymore. He is healed. God has given me strength—his strength. Right after the officer found him, I hit the floor; there was nothing left from the years of struggling with Gary's illness. I felt totally empty. It was the weakest, hollowest time of my life. Now each day I can feel God's strength in my life. It is amazing where he has taken me.

As a mom, this has been so hard. I can't fix the pain my children are feeling. I can't make this better for them. We have all hurt so much. For all of them, I am trying to reassure them all that Gary's death is not their fault at all. He made a choice. I am trying to teach them to be more compassionate to others and to each other. I am very verbal and open with them about mental illness and addiction—and the S word, *suicide*. Because when we talk about it, it takes the power away. I don't want them to walk in shame. Since everyone knows he died by suicide, we talk about his death and how it affects them. I am not afraid to use the word *suicide*. I want to be real with them and have them understand as much as they can. There will be no more secrets in our home. They are all angry and brokenhearted and embarrassed. They know loss now. They miss having their dad here for birthdays, school events, soccer games. Gary has never seen his daughter play basketball or soccer.

Because of Gary's decision that night, my kids are so angry; this is now pervasive in our home. We are working every day to come to grips with what happened and the loss they feel every day. My anger comes up now and again because I am a single parent again. I can't call Gary and share things about what the kids have accomplished or are having trouble with. They won't ever have their daddy watching them in the school play. He won't be there for our daughter's last day of elementary school or her first day of middle school. They won't have their dad to take them to Doughnuts for Dads breakfast at school. My youngest daughter isn't honest about where her daddy is when kids ask her. She tells them to be quiet and go away. God continues to give me peace, and I am praying that they gain that same peace.

My quiet time in the morning is my sanctuary. That one-on-one time with God is the resource I need for my day. People praying for me have given me strength that words cannot express. I am now realizing why God put the people in my life through the years when he did. Each one has spoken life and truth when I needed them. The role each one has played in my life over the past seven months has gotten me through to where I am today. This summer I got a part-time job at the lake serving coffee. I was blessed just in the first couple of days. Just watching godly people interact was a huge blessing to me, as was being at work and keeping my mind off of the troubles of my life. I got a reprieve there. There were also hints of healing that God had placed around. When Gary was working at that same lake, he planted 150 rosebushes. And it was tough the first few days to walk past the flowers and see the blooms, knowing that he had planted them but now is not here to see the blooms and their beauty. Now, I see that as a parallel with the kids—he is not here to see them blossom and bloom. It also showed me that although he is gone, my life will still keep growing and changing. The flowers he planted don't die because he is gone; they keep blooming and growing, just like our lives will keep blooming and growing, year after year. God is so good to remind me of these truths.

A few months later at the lake, I had an amazing experience. The Salvation Army did their yearly conference at our center, with about thirteen hundred people. I had an epiphany when I realized what the Salvation Army did in their recovery programs. I was serving the men who had walked through addiction and were on the other side. It gave me hope that people do get better. Recovery happens. I felt accepted by them before they even knew my story. That Wednesday evening, God pushed me to write my story down. I didn't want to write it; I kept putting it off. God kept on me to write, so finally, at ten o'clock that night, I started writing. The next day, God told me to take it to work. All day I was wondering what I was to do with it. My shift was almost over when I felt him tell me to give it to a lady who was in line. I had held the story all day waiting for God's direction. I gave her the story and told her to do with it whatever God led her to do. That night, I felt like I was supposed to be in the conference's evening meeting. God again was relentless about my attending that night. I went, and I sat in the back. The lady to whom I had given the story found me and shared how it had blessed her life. She asked my permission to read it to the group, and I agreed. There were several testimonies that night. At the end of the service, she read my story. She told everyone it was written by a coffee shop employee there at the lake. The next day was crazy—people kept asking me if I was the one who had written the story. They all expressed their condolences, said how the story had blessed them, and told me how deeply affected they were by it. They also expressed their prayers for our family this continued through Saturday morning. On Sunday, my family and I went to their service. The lady I had given the story to then gave me some CDs, DVDs, and a book.

She hinted many times that I could become a part of the Salvation Army Ministry. She said that when she asked some of the men how they knew that I had written the story, they answered with "It was the light on her face." God used that week to change my life. I had new energy and new life. For the first time since Gary died, I felt alive again. God had used these people and this experience to breathe life into my hurt, pain, and struggle. I immediately began speaking life into my children. I had hope and peace. Somehow I knew that, moving forward, instead of just surviving the day, I would thrive for the first time in years.

Since that week, I applied for a full-time job at the lake. I knew that is where God wanted me to be. I got the job about two months ago. They work with my schedule, as I'm a single mom raising my four children. I am where God wants me to be. For the first time in a long time, I get to go to work; I don't *have* to go to work. For the first time in over seven years, we took a family vacation provided by the generosity of others. We actually got to go to the beach; my youngest saw the ocean for the first time. For that week, I did not have to think of the chaos, pain, and constant strain. We got to just rest for the first time since Gary died.

Another amazing aspect of this time since Gary died has been the effect on his mom. Gary's mom was far from God. Over the years, she expressed that she was a pagan. I prayed for her often throughout the years. She really never seemed to want to listen. Going through this horrible experience with her and seeing her pain in losing her son, her only child, awakened something within her. Somewhere in the midst of her pain and suffering, she found hope in Jesus. Her big struggle through the years was being out of control. She constantly wanted to control every aspect of life. In the midst of losing her son, everything was completely out of her control. She realized that she was out of control and that God was the only one who could truly be in control of her life. Being able to let go of that control opened her heart to God for the first time. Over the past seven months, she has sought advice, watched sermons, and begun to listen to what God wants her to know. One particular sermon from NewSpring Church in South Carolina was David Blackburn's story about losing his wife through a home-invasion shooting. In that sermon, David advised that he had gotten through his tragedy by learning to run to the roar. He shared what he learned about how lions hunt. The male lion roars so that the prey runs away from him and toward the awaiting lionesses, which actually kill the prey. He advised that instead of running away from the roar of pain and suffering, we should run toward the roar. In running toward the pain instead of away from it, we find strength, courage, and the ability to overcome. Gary's mom is hungry to keep learning more about God and is going to church regularly.

When I reflect on the past twelve years of my marriage to Gary and how our relationship finally ended, I think about the Lord and where he has taken me since then. I was a single mother of two when Gary and I met in the summer of 2001. I wasn't saved. Even though I grew up in the church, I didn't have a relationship with Jesus Christ yet. I thought I needed to be rescued and saved, that I couldn't do life on my own. When I met Gary, he was my knight in shining armor. I didn't know who I was or what I wanted or where I was going. I did not know Jesus all that well. After two and a half years of overseas talking, we decided that we needed to be together and got married. I was still just as lost. Through the years of addiction and mental and verbal abuse, I still didn't know who I was. I felt like I was just going through the motions of life. There was always something—problems, trials, issues, hardship, trauma—some kind of chaos in our relationship and home. I was always trying to fix, cover up, and clean up all the messes that his illnesses created. In 2008, Gary and I both accepted Jesus into our hearts at a Vacation Bible School closing ceremony. I had peace, forgiveness, and importance for the first time in my life. The struggles went forward, but I had peace in my life. It was still hard. The messes were still there, and we went through some dark times, including rehab, separations, and confusion on the part of the children. Addiction and mental illness were putting such a strain on us both and our children. It was so hard to cope. Each day, I just wanted to survive and get better. In many ways, I was growing and learning to set boundaries. I was learning what it was truly like to trust in Jesus and to depend on him.

In some ways, since Gary died, I am still cleaning up his messes, fixing and covering for him. But for the first time, I am finding out who I am and what my purpose is, what plans God really has in my life. I would not wish the past seven months on anyone. But this is the journey I am on. This is the path that life has taken our family on, and God will use it for his glory. For the first time in my life, I know that I don't need to be rescued or saved. Jesus did that for me two thousand years ago. I wish both Gary and I had truly discovered that earlier. Now, I am letting Him guide my life and my path by His direction instead of doing it my way. It really is the only way to live.

So my prayer for you, for anyone who is on a path similar to mine, is that you will hang onto Jesus. He has already rescued you. He has the strength when you are weak. He has a plan to take this mess and make it beautiful. If you don't know Jesus or don't have a relationship with him, it is my prayer that you would ask him to be Lord of your life. It has made all the difference in my life, my children's lives, Gary's mom's life, and my parents' lives. Because a great friend of ours invited us to her church just to watch our kids at their VBS program, I know that my husband is in heaven where he will spend eternity with Jesus and that one day we will all meet him there. I would not have made it this far without the provisions that God had in store before Gary chose to take his life. He already provided what you need before your loved one left you. He will continue to provide. What was meant for evil, Jesus alone can use for our good and for the good of others. I have also learned a saying from my Alcoholics Anonymous friends: "1. I did not cause it. 2. I can't control it. 3. I can't cure it." I know deep in my soul that God has allowed all the pain in our lives for a reason—to use it to help others and to glorify him! If I can share my story and it can help someone, then I want him to use it! I am a child of God. I pray that you too will find that comfort and peace that God graciously gives every day!

Journal Opportunity

What do you miss?

_____

_____

_____

_____

_____

Share a special memory of your loved one.

_____

_____

_____

_____

_____

_____

Share an ordinary, everyday kind of memory of your loved one.

_____

_____

_____

_____

_____

_____

What hope did you gain from Cheri's story?

_____

_____

_____

_____

_____

_____

Chapter 9

What They Will Miss

I think this is the hardest part for me. I was twenty-three when my dad decided to leave us, and now he has missed a lot! He has never gotten to meet my kids or his other granddaughter. He would have loved them. He now has a grandson, who looks a lot like he did as a kid. My daughter loves Dunkin' Donuts, maybe more than my dad did. She would have loved to go with her grandpa on a Saturday morning and eat doughnuts with him. He loved being a grandpa.

Dad will never get to take my kids to the park, take them snowmobiling, or eat doughnuts together. He will never see them play soccer or perform in a school program. He didn't get to hold them when they were babies. He never saw them crawl or walk or listen to one of their stories. He didn't get to spoil them at the store. He didn't get to fuss at me about what I wasn't doing right. He has already missed a lot, and he will miss more—graduations, weddings, great-grandchildren, successes, losses, dreams fulfilled. He will also miss watching his legacy unfold before his eyes.

In my eighteen-year journey since my dad left us, this is the hardest point. He has missed so much. I know life is hard and he didn't feel he could go on, but there sure was a lot of life left for him to experience. Yes, I have been angry, hurt, frustrated, sad, and devastated. But most of all, he missed out on so many memories. He was *not* thinking about all the things he would miss out on in that moment that he ended his life. I know that if he had really thought it out—as hard as it seemed at the time—he would have made a different choice, because even with all the hardships in life, there is always good awaiting us around the next corner.

This is another area about grief that will come in waves. You will be sitting at a baseball field and a wave of recognition will happen—the recognition that someone is missing. All those feelings may come up again. The anger, frustration, and sadness may arise again as you realize how much you miss that someone. Then there are the other people in your life who are also feeling all these things at different stages who may continue to complicate your journey. Remember, this is a journey. Your relatives and friends will be at different stages at different times on their own journeys. Different waves will hit them at different times. Give one another a lot of grace. Everyone grieves at a different pace. You cannot make someone grieve. Some people get stuck in their grief. They are unable to move forward, to take the steps we have been talking about. Others avoid the whole process, like they don't even acknowledge what happened or the loss of someone significant in their lives. Some people focus so much on the loss that they are immersed in it and become stagnant, if living at all.

A journey is just that. There will be good days and difficult days. There will be moments when your heart is broken in a thousand pieces. Then there will be other days that just feel good, normal even. On your journey, the goal is to keep moving forward, making progress a little bit at a time. Some days you regress; some days you push forward. When you keep moving, everything seems to stay in balance. That is what our loved ones lost sight of. They got stuck instead of moving forward.

Also recognize that if your loved one had been struggling for years from a mental health issue, a physical disability, or an addiction, he or she is free. There is no more struggling. So our loved ones are missing the struggle as well. They are not going to miss the pain, struggle, and sometimes humility that came with their illnesses (if they had one). They will not miss that pain. You may at times feel a peace about this, and that is okay. It is your journey. You may have been suffering right alongside them. They are free, and so are you. Let this peace cover you. Let God cover you with the peace that passes all understanding.

Your loved one will miss a lot. But if we do grieve well, if we really heal and allow God's love and peace to wash over us, a part of them will come with us. They have been a very vibrant part of our lives. They have impacted us, changed us, and shaped us. How could they not continue on our journey with us? We hold their memory. We can honor them every day forward from here.

Journal Opportunity

What do you think your loved one is missing right now in this season of life? What do you think he or she will miss as life moves forward?

_____

_____

_____

_____

_____

_____

_____

What memories or thoughts do you want to take with you from your loved one?

_____

_____

_____

_____

_____

_____

_____

Chapter 10

Remembering and Living a Legacy

No matter what your relationship was with your loved one, you have two things to do as you move forward: (1) remember him or her and (2) live a life that would honor your loved one and make him or her proud.

We are our loved ones' legacy. We are the ones left to make a difference, finish the work, and change the world. In the midst of their pain, suffering, distorted thinking, and brokenness, our loved ones made a choice—a choice that altered us forever. That one decision has shaken us to our cores. It is different than other deaths. It is not the way you wanted or planned, but there is a tomorrow. I know because I have walked out of that valley. And I have walked with other people out of that valley. I have witnessed God do miraculous things in, through, and around people whose lives suicide has touched. I have seen God provide, heal, and mend hearts. He has mended mine. There is hope. There is peace.

A New Normal

We have to start a new normal. We have to put one foot in front of the other. It is not what we chose, but it is what we have to deal with.

The reality is that we now have a choice. We can collapse into our pain and sorrow. We can set up camp and live in the valley of the shadow of death. We can allow our own mental health and addictions to take over. We can keep both feet in the past and not move forward. We all have choices. You have a choice. I have a choice. Sometimes you will have to make this choice a thousand times a day.

We can make the choice. We can remember him. We can remember her. We can keep living. I am my father's legacy. My children are my father's legacy. My brother, my nieces— we are all my father's legacy. How I treat others and the choices I make are a reflection of him. I hope he would be proud. I hope he knows how much I love and miss him. I hope he knows I will cherish the memories I did have with him. I hope your loved one will too!

My scrapbook helped me heal. It allowed me to put my memories down on paper so that my kids would know their grandpa. It helped me go through the grief process and allows me to keep his memory alive. I have pictures on my wall that are in a spot just for me. I carry my dad's army dog tags on my keychain, just the way he did. I remember—how could I forget? Sometimes I remember happy things, and sometimes the memories sadden me still. But I am healed. I can love and serve others. I have purpose, meaning, and peace in my life. My heart's desire is that you will find this peace too.

The Bible is clear: God is big enough to help you through this. He is present enough for you to never be alone. He is generous enough to meet the need you have right now. He has the healing you need. He will never grow weary of your asking. He loves you so much.

What Is Your Legacy?

Live a legacy that you and your loved one will be proud of. I encourage you to live life without regrets and live life giving hope to others. Start tearing down the stigma around mental health and addiction problems. The more we talk about these issues and the more people feel a part of their communities, the more lives that will be saved. Mental illness and addiction are real diseases. They are also treatable diseases. Be honest, share your story, and share your loved one's story. My dad is gone. But his memory is strong if one person is helped by his story. Build communities by being an active part of sports groups, churches, and community centers. Give back to others around you. Every single suicide is a tragedy—Every. Single. One. Let's work together to reach out to the hurting in our communities. Let people reach out to you! Tell people what you need when a need arises.

A few years after my dad died, God gave me my calling. He gave me a couple of verses that set the course for my life and brought healing to my soul. Hebrews 12:12–13 says, "Therefore, strengthen your feeble arms and weak knees. Make level paths for your feet. So that the lame may not be disabled, but rather healed." God strengthened my feeble arms and weak knees, and by his grace I have witnessed others' healing from so many things that held them back. I have been healed, and to God's glory, so can you! My prayer is this: pour out your heart and soul to Jesus. He is your Savior, your comfort, and your healing. Then find good people to support you, pack up camp, and start walking out of your valley. God will heal us and lead us into tomorrow. He has this promise for us in Jeremiah 29:11: "'For I know the plans I have for you,' declares the Lord, 'plans to prosper you and not to harm you, plans to give you a hope and a future.'"

Our futures are our loved ones' legacies. Today we begin grieving and healing. Then we take the first step to remember and live the legacy God has given us to live. Today, we choose to walk, one step at a time, out of the valley and into the light!

Journal Opportunity

What is your loved one's legacy? Begin writing his or her story.

_____

_____

_____

_____

_____

_____

Chapter 11

There Is a Time

I love living in the mountains for many reasons, but one of the most obvious is the beautiful seasons we experience. Fall is my favorite season. All the leaves change into dramatic shades of orange, yellow, and red; there is a cool, crisp bite in the air; and the smells of pumpkin, spice, and apples seem to be everywhere. Summer is over, things start dying off, and the harvest is collected. Change is coming. Then there is a transition into winter. It is cold, and time is spent indoors. It is time to be still, to wait out a snowstorm, to see the sun glisten off of the snow-drenched treetops. All the growth of summer is completely dormant, resting, taking a well-earned break. Then, gradually, things start warming, and yet another transition begins. Birds come back, trees start blooming, flowers begin to show color, and green appears everywhere. The sun seems to start gently warming away the harshness of winter. Spring arrives— change is coming again. It is new life, new birth, almost like the earth is awaking. Spring brings forth life, and then summer grows that life to its potential. Summer, glorious summer, is back with the rest and busyness all at the same time. We are active outside, soaking up sunshine. We gather at pools, lakes, and rivers. It really is rarely terribly hot in the mountains, so summer is amazing here! All the seasons are amazing. All the seasons have their joys and struggles. The key is enjoying what you can and recognizing that change will come.

I think life is much like seasons. I know that I have gone through many seasons in life. In fact, I am in the middle of one now. I would rather not go back to some seasons, but some have made me stronger. I have enjoyed every moment of some of them. But each season has its purpose. Each season needs to come, maybe so we can appreciate the joys and the sorrows of another season. Each season has joys and sorrows in it. Each season has a lesson embedded in it. What is different from the natural seasons is that I believe God can keep us in a season until we have received what we needed. Sometimes we stay in a season far longer than God ever intended because we refuse to do what God desires for us to do. Sometimes we stay in the valley when God has a mountaintop for us to explore. I do know that this season of darkness we go through when a loved one dies is not intended forever. It is a season. But it is a necessary season that we go through. I think some people try to avoid this season altogether. They decide to just get busy, avoid the pain, and press on. While this seems to work on the outside, it is rarely what our souls really need. The Lord reminded me of some great truths recently about the seasons in our lives. Take a moment and really allow these words to sink into your soul. Apply this passage to whatever season of life you are in.

There is a time for everything, and a season
for every activity under heaven:
A time to be born and a time to die,
A time to plant and a time to uproot,
A time to kill and a time to heal,
A time to tear down and a time to build,
A time to weep and a time to laugh,
A time to mourn and a time to dance,
A time to scatter stones and a time to gather
them,
A time to embrace and a time to refrain,
A time to search and a time to give up,
A time to keep and a time to throw away,
A time to tear and a time to mend,
A time to be silent and a time to speak,
A time to love and a time to hate,
A time for war and a time for peace.

What does the worker gain from his toil? I
have seen the burden God has laid on men.
He has made everything beautiful in its time.
He has also set eternity in the hearts of men;
yet they cannot fathom what God has done
from beginning to end. I know that there
is nothing better for men than to be happy
and do good while they live. That everyone
may eat and drink and find satisfaction in all
his toil—this is a gift from God. I know that
everything God does will endure forever;
nothing can be added to it and nothing taken
away from it. God does it so that men will
revere him. (Ecc. 3:1–14)

In grief, we will go through these seasons. There is a time to mourn and a time to dance. There is a time to keep and a time to throw away. There is a time to tear and a time to mend. There is a time to weep and a time to laugh. There is a time to be silent and a time to speak. There is a time to tear down and a time to build. Here is the key: just like the natural seasons, we must go through these seasons of life. We need new growth and times of growing. We need times to let go, relax, and be released from the pain. There are times of rest and dormancy. This is all the balance and beauty of life. Let your grief come and see it for what it is, a natural season of life. Spring will come again. Laughter will fill the air, and dancing will come. God knows our hearts. We are created in his image. Hear his message through this passage. He sets eternity in our hearts. He makes everything beautiful in his time. He will endure forever, and nothing can be taken away from him. Whatever season you are in, he wants you to revere him. The beautiful part of this truth is that God is in and through every season of your life. Don't rush through a season you need more time in, and don't linger longer than he desires.

Austin's Story

I wanted to share a story about these seasons of life. My friend Austin allowed me to interview him to share his story and his very long season of alcohol addiction. I also thought it might help to hear a story of someone who was on the brink of suicide and what led him up to that desperate place. Sometimes hearing someone's thought process can help bring understanding. Austin is someone I have had the privilege to get to know through my church. He has strength, courage, and passion. He has also been in a very dark place. He wanted you to know what led him to the darkness and how he got through his valley. Here is his story.

Growing up, life in the mountains was great. I grew up playing in the river, hiking, and fishing. I was an only child and enjoyed a great relationship with both of my parents. I was blessed to live across the hill from my paternal grandparents and just a few miles from my maternal grandparents. I was surrounded by a loving, attentive family. We experienced the normal ups and downs in life.

I had a very close relationship with my dad, like a brother. We played, talked, and genuinely enjoyed hanging out. My mom has always been a rock in my life, unmovable and the constant voice of reason.

I was a really great kid growing up—involved in sports, won citizenship awards, had lots of friends, and had always been involved in church. I remember when I was nine years old I asked Jesus into my heart at a revival at Mt. Zion Baptist Church. On a Sunday years later, I will never forget what the pastor there, Heath, spoke over me on the way out the door—"God has great things in store for you." Those words would come back just when I needed to hear them.

I grew up in rural Western North Carolina. So tobacco grows well here, and I remember experimenting once with cigarettes early on. I remember feeling so guilty about it. It was quite a while until I tried another one. Then the summer before my freshman year of school, I got drunk with a buddy of mine and I got sick—real sick. It was not a great experience, so again, I stepped back and didn't drink for a while. But by the fall of my freshman year I was doing what I thought every teenage kid does and started experimenting and drinking after Friday night football games. For me, it was the high school party scene. I figured everyone did it. I really did not drink much that first year. Over the high school years, I started drinking more and more. I have to admit, I was having fun but I learned early on to hide what I was doing—learning skills that would play a significant role later in my life. I was still a "good kid"; I kept up my involvement in sports and church, and my loving, attentive family were unaware of these extracurricular activities.

By the time I graduated high school, I was socially conditioned to drink, right in time for college. Before the first day of classes I earned my first underage drinking ticket. I continued to do what I thought all college students do. I went to classes, did well. When I wasn't in class or studying, I partied. It wasn't too bad the first couple years. Then my junior year, I started living off campus. That is when alcohol became pretty important in my life. Marijuana and alcohol were now an everyday part of my life. I began needing to have it. Looking back, I can see it was a problem. Back then I thought I was just having a good time. I maintained my good-kid status with academic success, keeping an A-B average, and always involved in church. I even had a six- to eight-month period of time that I felt convicted and got right with God and was passionate for him for a little while. That quickly faded, and I was back drinking. By the last year in college, I was drinking a lot.

After graduating college, I lived by myself and worked in construction. I continued my drinking lifestyle. At this point, drinking became a part of functioning. It was in all my social situations; I would provide it if I needed to. I was trying to balance my professional career and the college lifestyle at the same time. Then in 2009, the economy took a dip and I got laid off. Around the same time, I reunited with a childhood friend and we started dating. I was scared of commitment at the time, but I knew she was the one. We would drink together, but our drinking was always different. She never had a problem and never seemed to be intoxicated. I always seemed to overdo my drinking.

When I found out that jobs were becoming available, I got convicted about marijuana. I prayed a lot and felt like God took that from me. I really never struggled with giving up marijuana. I landed a good, solid job that drug tested and I was doing pretty well, but there was still drinking.

I asked that childhood friend to marry me. We were about a month out from getting married, and I got a DWI. That was an eye opener, not as much for me as it was for my friends and family that I had a problem with alcohol. The wedding was almost called off, but with the promise to quit drinking, everything was put back into place. This was the first of many attempts to quit drinking. The positive thing at the time was that I was exposed to AA meetings, although only as a scoffer, meaning I was there but did not really buy into the program. I basically said what I needed to get out of my situation but did not really make any changes. I did not make it even to a sixty-day chip. I completed my DWI assessment and required treatment. With no license and soon to be married, I felt a lot of judgment. I was sober for my wedding. But after each new incident, I would make short-lived amends with others and myself, and then I would get comfortable and go back to drinking.

During the newlywed season of my life, there were good times and then bad times. It seemed to be up and down all the time. I had some incidents that I really showed out with my drinking in front of my wife's friends; I am still working on making amends for these. Progressively, drinking became all the time, except at work. If I wasn't at work, I had to drink. It became compulsive. I had to have it.

I was still involved in church and enjoyed a great church family. I was a good employee, and I kept my wife and family in the dark with my drinking as much as possible.

Then I had a son. I knew that my wife needed my help. She became more resistant about my drinking and did not allow alcohol in the house. So I had to get myself in check. For a while, I did and did not cause any major problems with my drinking. I was living a lie, though. I was angry, and I realized I became selfish—I was protecting my alcohol above all else, even my wife and my son. I distanced myself from my wife and anyone who did not agree with my drinking.

Over the next year, my drinking got really bad. I was binging out all the time. Alcohol became a monster in my life. I did not know myself without alcohol. I did not know who I was if I wasn't drinking. My social life was completely consumed by alcohol. I only wanted to hang out with people if we could drink together and they approved of my drinking. It became who I was. Lies compounded constantly. It became hard to keep up with what I had told everyone. My wife kept asking me over and over what I had done, who I had been with—I could not remember where I was and what I did. Depression began to set in. I was in constant anxiety about the lies. The women in my life would call me out on it. My wife and mom could smell the alcohol on me. I was so insecure. My insecurities really came out when I was around successful people, so I would be the fun one at the party. Then, because of the issues I created by partying (when the drinking crossed the line from fun to destructive), my social relationships became very strained. So then I started increasingly drinking in secret. I quickly became a closet drinker. Somehow what once gave me confidence, fun, and excitement now was providing a life of solitude, isolation, and depression.

I was not happy without my alcohol. I was miserable all day, waiting to drink when I got off work. My relationships were stained.

I did not know how to relate to anyone unless I was intoxicated. I would ask, *Why can't I be a normal person and drink normally?* I knew just how much I needed to drink to get right where I needed it to be to function socially. Then if the social situation changed, I would want more and more, causing even more problems.

Trust was gone in my relationships—with my wife, my mom, and many other family and friends. Honestly, no one was more deceived than I was. I had come to the point that *this* is who I was. I believed I would eventually slip up and lose it all. My history showed that I would mess up again. I was good at the lies and pretending to be whatever everyone wanted me to be. But when I saw myself, I was less than others. Things quickly spiraled out of control. When something happened, I was so hard on myself. I knew the Lord was working on me. I would only pray for my family. But I never prayed for myself—I never engaged in a conversation with God. I isolated myself from even God. Then I began to question my salvation: *If I am saved, how did I become this guy?* Sundays got hard. The conviction of sitting in church and hearing truth was overwhelming. I wanted to drink. When I look back, there were people who believed in me that kept speaking truth. At the time, I ignored them, but their words were in my soul.

One Sunday, I saw a small group in my church that was for people who were struggling with mental health or substance abuse issues. So I went.

On February 18, 2015, everything came to a head. I had thought about suicide as a passing thought previously. But it was nothing I had considered before. It was a cold day. My wife called and said she and her mom had agreed that it would be good for her and our son to stay at her mom's house because of the weather. Of course I agreed. What was my first thought? I was going to have a bachelor's night—drinking with different friends. I did not drink a ridiculous amount, knowing I needed to get home. My wife called, and she heard it in my voice. I finally admitted to her that I had been drinking. She responded with "I don't want to talk to you. I am tired of this." I tried to reason this out. I said to myself, *I will fix this with her in a little while.* But then I went into a depressed rage. I became very critical of myself, to the point of self-loathing. By this time, I was at home in the middle of my rage, and I found myself in a pit. I went and got a gun from my dresser and laid it on the coffee table. Then, in my drunken mind, I went through a systematic process of questions: *Where do I want to be found? What do I want my last words to be?* Then I began beating myself up: *I am a terrible dad and husband. They are better off without me.* I was methodically thinking my own suicide through. I looked up at the ceiling and asked God directly, "What do you want from me?" I allowed that door to God to open again. I was screaming at God about all my failures, ranting and raving to God. At the end of my rant, I felt an undeniable peace. I started hearing the words that were in my soul from the many who had believed in me and spoken truth to me—Lee's voice, my first small group leader at church; Tim's voice, a missionary God had put in my path; Rupert's voice, a friend who had gotten sober six months previous; stories from the meetings of the twelve steps; and Heath's voice, saying, "God has great things in store for you." I started seeing my wife and son for what they were. The whirlwind went from 120 miles per hour to a peaceful breeze on the beach. I had peace for the first time. I called all the men who had reached out to me. I was still intoxicated, but I called them for help. I told them I would get into AA. I called my wife and made promises that I had made before, but this time I meant it.

I don't know why I turned to God in that moment. I wish I knew. Since then I have lost friends to suicide. I understand being that desperate. I understand the desperation that led me to getting the gun out and planning my own death. I would not wish any of this desperation on anyone, but I know so many people struggle with it.

The next morning, I woke up and knew I was going to break all the promises I had made. I regretted making all those promises. I felt like there was no way I could stop my alcohol use. I had been drinking half my life. By the time I got off work, I was sick to my stomach. My wife came in and confronted me about not being at AA and lying again. Begrudgingly, I went to my first meeting, and then I continued on to 160 meetings in 160 days. I started praying, fervently. For the first time in my life, I put everything in my being into my prayers. AA provided the accountability for me. The first two days, my thoughts were about alcohol, but by day three, I started thinking more about recovery. And by God's grace, day three was the last time I craved alcohol. Then I started walking out my recovery. AA helped me so much. My one-year medallion is always with me. My recovery is focused on giving back. I am active in my church, not just present. I am transparent about the disease that I still have. I am helping others; I am sharing my story. It is scary to look back on it. Anxiety sometimes creeps in and scares me. There are times of weakness, not about alcohol but my anxieties. Who do I think I am to help other people? The things I do today are what keep me sober. I am still working the steps; I am helping people find recovery. I have balance in my life. I help provide a way for people to get out of their desperation, where I had been that cold February night. I lead a men's group in my church—helping others, holding one another accountable. It is harder now than it ever has been because I am involved in the fight. It is a true and honest fight. It goes better now because I am a much stronger person than I was. I crawled in the ditch for so long and would not look up. I knew God was there; I just would not let him influence me. I am still learning to rewire how I think, how to be an adult, how to be a man in ministry, a true father, husband, friend, son, and grandson. It is hard, but I rest when God provides rest. God prepares me for the work he has for me. The key for me is listening to God and obeying the spirit when he leads. The sanctification has been unreal. I know my thought process has not healed. But one day at a time, I am enjoying the harvest of the new seeds I am sowing. Recovery is hard work, but it is so worth it.

The truth is there is a lot of scar tissue in my marriage and my relationships. I was not the only person affected by my alcohol, depression, and anxiety. I still have a long way to go, but I feel we have our trust back. We have been blessed with another son. We are learning to be parents together. We are learning each day at a time to live, learn, love, and depend on God. I am so thankful for the men that God put in my life over the years. I am thankful for faithful churches and pastors who proclaim truth Sunday after Sunday. I am thankful for AA, for accountability, and for recovery. What I have learned is that we need to speak truth over others, even if they don't want to hear it. Those words can come back and make a difference. I know not everyone's story ended like mine. I too have lost good friends to suicide. I know the pain of holding a loved one when they have just heard the tragic news of their death of their son, father, friend. It is a dark place. But fight the fight. God has put you in this fight—don't back down. Keep your eyes on him, and he will strengthen you and give you what you need one day at a time.

Journal Opportunity

What season of life are you in?

_____

_____

_____

Austin shared about his addiction and the thoughts and life circumstances that led him to wanting to commit suicide. How did his story affect you? What understanding, if any, did you gain of your own loved one's thought patterns?

_____

_____

_____

_____

_____

_____

Austin took the negative in his life and is learning to help others because he understands what they are going through. When you are ready, how do you feel God is leading you to help others?

_____

_____

_____

_____

_____

_____

Chapter 12

Your Next Step

Thank you for coming on this journey with me. It is not a journey that we would have ever chosen to take, but here we are. I don't know where you are in this journey. You may still be in shock that your loved one is gone. You may be really angry right now—angry at your loved one, at God, or at yourself. You may be just sad, even depressed. You may feel completely unsettled, lost even. You may feel numb. You may have coped in unhealthy ways just so you did not have to feel the pain of the loss. You may be suffering in your own pit of despair.

You may be further along in this journey and at a place where you can begin to heal. You may have done many of the steps we have talked about together. You may even feel guilty for moving forward. Maybe it has been years since your loved one left you, and you still feel the tremendous hole in your life. It may be time to heal. Healing does not happen accidentally. Time doesn't actually heal us. We must be intentional and purposeful. We need to let our feelings come out in a healthy way. We need to spend time feeling the pain so we can purposely let it go.

Often in counseling over the years, I have used my backpack illustration. I imagine that everyone has a backpack that we carry around every day. It is with us all the time. When some incident occurs, a new brick forms within our souls. Depending on how severe the incident is, several bricks may form. These bricks are then deposited in our backpacks. We are walking around with our loads. Then something else happens, and we add some more bricks to our load. In time, we just get used to the loads we carry. We think it is the burden we must bear. Why? We were not meant to carry these heavy loads.

Matthew 11:28–29 says, "Come to me all you who are weary and burdened and I will give you rest. Take my yoke upon you and learn from me, for I am gentle and humble in heart and you will find rest for your souls. For my yoke is easy and my burden is light."

God never intended for us to carry these heavy loads. He never intended for us to have so many bricks in our backpacks. He came so that we would find rest. He came so that we would have life and have it to the full (John 10:10).

Your Next Step

So what is your next step? You have information now to help you heal. Maybe you think, *I don't have the hope that you have. I don't have that kind of relationship with God.* You can. God sent his son to earth to be the ultimate sacrifice for our sin, pain, and suffering. He knew the pain that sin would cause. When Adam and Eve sinned, he knew he would have to do something, and he did the unbelievable. He sent his son to pay the price for our sins. In doing this, he fulfilled his nature of holiness and mercy. He made this sacrifice to give us hope. He gave us options. He took our burdens and our sins on himself so we could have his "easy and light" burden. Salvation isn't just salvation from our sins; it is salvation from hopelessness, despair, and regret. That doesn't mean that we won't experience pain; quite obviously we do. But God provides a way through that pain. We will have our valleys. We may be in one now. But Jesus provides the way through the valleys. We have to make the choice to follow him out. Jesus offers hope. He voluntarily took your burden of sin. He is volunteering right now to take your burden of pain. You just need to ask him. If you don't know how, here is a simple prayer: "My Father, I know that I am a sinner. I believe that Jesus paid the price for my sins and my pain. I confess to you now that I cannot go through this life without you. I am surrendering my life to you."

If you made this decision today, I am so excited for you. It is literally the best decision you could ever make. Please tell someone today. You have a new family now. It is important that you spend time with your Father in heaven through prayer and his word, the Bible. It is also important to find a good church family to connect to for worship and fellowship.

Coming Back

Your next step may be coming back to God. You know you are his child, but losing your loved one to suicide has made you angry and pained, and you ran from God instead of toward him. Your next step may be having a hard conversation with God. He promises to never leave or forsake you. He can handle whatever you throw at him. He really is big enough. Go to him. Spend time with him. One story of someone I have worked with that comes to mind is about a young man who was angry as a result of childhood abuse. He had spent some time in a children's home. He was a Christian, but because of all the stuff he had gone through, he had disconnected from God. He asked all the same questions you and I have or are asking right now: How could God have let this happen? Why me? Why now? Does God really love me? Is God really out there? He discovered that the answer to the last two questions was yes. Over a series of events, God kept reminding him of truth. He said, "Three people have told me the exact same thing over the past week. Is that a coincidence?" Of course not. This truth opened his heart. He started talking to God again. Slowly he began to trust God again. He began to heal. God has never left you. He has always been there. He is waiting for you now. Your next step may be having a conversation with God again.

Let It Go

Your next step may be purging. In much the same way as we do spring cleaning, we need to do an emotional, spiritual, and sometimes physical purging. What are you holding onto that you need to let go of? While we need to hold onto the memories, sometimes stuff can clutter our souls, hearts, and homes. I chose to keep my dad's dog tags. I carry them on my keychain just like he did. I also have some pictures. My house is not overrun with his things, though. I kept what was important to me, and I let go of what was not. Many times I encourage people to keep a memory box. It can be a special box to keep letters and memorabilia—whatever helps you remember and honor your loved one. But it needs to fit in the box. If it doesn't, consider letting some things go. This is a process. Sometimes I go into people's homes and it is like their loved one is still there, with clothes in the closet and a coat hanging on the coat rack. Sometimes, their person's bedroom is just the way he or she left it years later. We need to let their things go. My daughter loved *Frozen* when it came out; we saw it three times in the theatre, and each time I sat there with tears running down my face. There is a powerful song in the movie, "Let It Go." It is beautifully performed. But I think the underlying message is one that is very powerful for young and old alike. Like Elsa, we have been holding onto something powerful that has been holding us back or controlling our daily lives. When we learn to let it go, there is freedom that allows us to be who God created us to be. Is your next step a physical purge? Do you need to let some things go that might quite literally be cluttering and holding you back?

Your next step may be an emotional purge. Are you the strong one? Has everyone depended on you to get through this situation? Have you had time just to cry, to feel all the rush of emotions? I had a college professor who shared a story of when she was working on her doctorate. In the middle of her doctoral thesis, her mother became ill and died. There were critical deadlines in her thesis, and if she did not complete them as expected and anticipated by her professors, her career would be put on hold. So she showed up to the funeral and then went straight back to work. She literally put her mother's death out of her mind so she could finish her work. Then, when she was done with her thesis and had officially earned her doctorate, she took several months to just grieve. She almost collapsed with it. She felt that she had to be strong, get through what she needed to get through, and then allow herself to grieve. But she knew she had to grieve at some point (her doctorate was in psychology). You may feel like everyone is depending on you so you cannot be weak. There is not a right or wrong way to have this catharsis—cry, mourn, wail, scream, run, craft, journal, exercise, scrapbook; do whatever it takes to let it go emotionally. My husband was very productive with his grief when his father had an inoperable brain tumor. As he watched his father decline, he was feeling his own pain. So what did he do? He chopped wood. I knew why he was out there. He spent hours chopping. We had plenty of wood that year. Sometimes emotions need a physical release, especially for men.

Connection

Maybe your next step is connection. If you have isolated yourself or pushed others away from you, it may be time to reconnect. You may have disconnected because you think that no one else knows or understands how you feel. You may be right. Each situation is unique; however, you are not alone. I know the word *suicide* scares the vast majority of people. But there are more people out there who can at least identify with you. There are more than you know, more than you think. It is time to reach out and try to connect with someone. I cannot promise you that you won't be hurt again. Relationships are inherently risky. But I can promise you that isolation will keep you in this valley.

Here are some ideas to help you connect with others:

- Attend a church
- Get involved in a small group
- Go to a club/group of a hobby or interest you enjoy
- Find a grief group
- Volunteer at a local nonprofit
- Meet a friend for a walk regularly
- Take a neighbor some cookies
- Get a pet
- Take a class
- Start a dinner club
- Get a fun part-time job

When it comes to connection, I think of a wagon wheel. When you are hurting, you don't want to rely just on one or two spokes. You want to have an entire wheel of supports with lots and lots of spokes. If you put all your help in one person or activity and something happens to that spoke, then you are going to stop rolling. You need a full wagon wheel with a lot of supports so you can keep on rolling out of this valley.

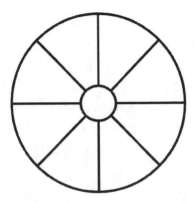

So who are your supports? For each spoke on this wheel, write a name or a resource that you have right now. For any empty spots, I challenge you to find things to start filling in the blanks. Connection is so important for healing. You don't always have to be strong. Everyone needs someone to lean on. This may be your next step out of the valley.

Professional Help

Sometimes we need a little help getting started on a journey. There are great counselors out there who specialize in grief, addiction, mental health issues, family issues, and crisis. You do not have to suffer in isolation. Counseling is really so helpful for so many people who are just stuck. In situations where our loved ones died by their own hand, we may need that extra support. Counseling is all about the relationship, so if you don't connect with someone at first, don't be afraid to find someone else. Group therapy is also very effective to build community and gain support with a professional leader guiding the group.

You may be at the point that your grief, pain, or isolation is physically affecting your body and brain. This is very common in intense grief situations. Many times, the chemicals in our brains can be affected with a significant loss. We may need medications for a time period to allow our brains and bodies to acclimate to our new circumstances. If you are opposed to medications, ask your physician or medical provider about vitamins, supplements, or holistic methods to find a physical balance. This is an important step to getting your body, brain, and emotions back to homeostasis, or balance. We all need balance in our lives, and such a loss can throw us off balance. You need to find that balance again. Professional help can be a helpful tool in attaining that balance.

Another complication in a suicide is if you were the one who found your loved one. That in and of itself can be traumatic and very difficult to integrate into your thought process and feelings. You had a horrible experience with someone you loved. This is considered to be a traumatic event. If you have recurrent dreams, hypervigilance, blunted emotions, and feel some disconnection because of the trauma you experienced, then you need to seek professional help. A trauma disorder could develop. It is so important that you seek help if you are struggling with trauma symptoms. Therapy with someone who specializes in trauma is so important to help you on your journey out of the valley.

Step Out of Addiction

Sometimes addiction can be subtle. Your loved one is gone, you are hurting, and you feel like you are in a deep pit. You just want the pain to stop. You take a drink or smoke a joint so that, for a little while, you don't have to feel anything. You are looking for some kind of relief. It is easy to turn to drugs, alcohol, and even over-the-counter medications. In time, what brought relief for a moment may become your new best friend. Slowly, you need more and more of this new friend to bring the relief you once felt. The problems that you are running from are still there, and now there may be more. While your new best friend is always there for you and you can always count on it (substance or behavior) for relief, it may be causing more problems than it solves. But how do you let it go now? You need it—desperately. You try to distance yourself, but now you can't. You have to have it.

Addiction starts this way. I cannot tell you the countless stories of people who have turned to alcohol and drugs to cope with a loss. I can tell you that alcohol and drugs never cure your pain. They never bring healing. Temporarily they bring a false sense of relief, but it is not real. It is a trap.

I want to share a story of someone I worked with. He was someone who enjoyed a cold beer after work. Then, tragedy struck. His sweet, four-year-old son died tragically because of someone else's lackadaisical care. His pain and grief became unmanageable, and he turned to alcohol. It became his best friend for years. His story does not end well. He lost his wife, his business, his home, and his health. Do not turn to substances or addictive behaviors in your grief. That is not the time to drown your sorrows. I have heard far too many stories of pain. I want your story to be one of hope, restoration, and God's amazing grace.

If you are already down this path and have turned to substances or behaviors like gambling, shopping, or eating to calm your grief, there is help. Please take that next step to professional help. Addiction never helped anyone grieve.

Your Story

Now it is time to write your story. Wherever you find yourself today, there is a next step. Whether you have been grieving for a few days or for decades, you don't have to stay where you are. It is time to begin taking one step after another to walk out of your valley. Whether your next step is to start a personal relationship with Jesus Christ, to come back to Jesus, to make some personal connections, to seek professional help, or to avoid or end your addictions, today is the day you can take your first step. I know it is not easy. It was not easy for me. But by the grace of God, I have walked through the valley my dad created. I have walked with people through the valleys that were created for them. I have seen miracles. I have hope that your story will glorify God and bring hope to others. Your loved one did not die in vain. Share your story. Today, start walking out of your valley into the light that God has for you. My God is big enough to meet you wherever you are. He is waiting to help you take your next step.

Works Cited

American Psychiatric Association. 2013. *Diagnostic and Statistical Manual of Mental Disorders.* 5th ed. Washington, DC: Author.

McCauley, Kevin. 2010. *Pleasure Unwoven: A Personal Journey about Addiction.* DVD. The Institute for Addiction Study.

NewSpring, Davey Blackburn interview.- http://daveyblackburn.com/posts/ interview-at-newspring-church

"Suicide Statistics." American Foundation for Suicide Prevention. https://afsp.org/about-suicide/suicide-statistics.

Resource List

Following is a list of resources for those who have lost a loved one to suicide or who may be contemplating suicide

1. American Association of Christian Counselors—Find counselors in your area: http://www.aacc.net/resources/find-a-counselor/
2. Suicide Prevention Hotline: http://www.suicidepreventionlifeline.org/
3. American Foundation for Suicide Prevention: https://afsp.org/find-support/ive-lost-someone/find-a-support-group/
4. Alliance of Hope: http://www.allianceofhope.org/
5. The Samaritans: http://samaritansnyc.org/
6. Support After Suicide: http://www.supportaftersuicide.org.au/

Printed in the United States
By Bookmasters